Now the Lord is the Spirit,
and where the Spirit of the Lord is,
there is freedom.

—2 CORINTHIANS 3:17

Here is what some of the church's greatest leaders have said about Jamie Buckingham...

Reminiscing on Jamie's life and ministry is like walking through a magnificent museum where marvels of accomplishment shine in seemingly endless array. When the history of our era is written, Jamie Buckingham's place will most certainly be noted with distinction—and with praise to God.

—JACK HAYFORD, PASTOR

Not long after Jamie and I worked together on my first book, I found out the only reason he had agreed to write it: The day he interviewed me he saw a hole in the bottom of my shoe. He never was impressed by glitz and glitter, but he figured if a former Baptist minister couldn't afford to have his shoes repaired, he must be for real.

—PAT ROBERTSON, BROADCASTER

Jamie touched multitudes of people, both those in the body of Christ and those not. He touched everyone, even children, with his uncommon sermons, his stories, his reminiscings—with his totally honest and unaffected approach.

—ORAL ROBERTS, HEALING EVANGELIST

Jamie had one of the more unique ministries of the 20th century: He was a pastor and elder to the whole church. He was a true stateman who left the church and the world better than he found it. He did not follow trends; he started them and gave courage to many others to boldly follow their vision.

—**RICK JOYNER**, PROPHETIC MINISTER

The church across all denominational lines needs to receive a fresh outpouring of the very life and love of God. Jamie demonstrated this reality in his brightest moments and in his darkest hours. His writing challenged me and often put a smile on my face. His life put joy in my soul and helped focus my attention on Jesus alone.

—**JAMES ROBISON**, EVANGELIST

Jamie ministered to multitudes for decades. He brought hope, humor, wisdom and spiritual life to all of us. These things and the ministry that he founded will live on and affect the whole world.

—**LOREN CUNNINGHAM**, EVANGELIST

One of Christianity's mightiest pens was stilled when Jamie died. His voice was powerful and relevant. He spoke with authority but without arrogance, always speaking the truth in love. His voice will speak in a thousand ways for years to come, through his books, articles and recorded works. No one will take his place.

—**JACK TAYLOR**, MINISTER

The energy Jamie possessed always astonished me. He regularly packed a day and a half into a single day. I'm convinced Jamie, perhaps like none other, packed a century of life into his 60 years.

—**JOHN SHERRILL**, AUTHOR

Jamie has been one of the greatest prophetic voices to our generation in the church. His greater testimony is that he was a man of God first and a minister second.

—**BILL HAMON**, BISHOP

The first time Jamie Buckingham came to our church, I introduced him to my congregation as one of the world's foremost Christian authors and original thinkers. They fell in love with this unorthodox apostle of the charismatic movement.

—**JOHN HAGEE**, PASTOR

Jamie spoke for us all. His candor, humor and, above all, his integrity made his commentaries extremely valuable for his contemporaries. He spoke also to future generations. He will be quoted by future historians to the end of time.

—**VINSON SYNAN**, HISTORIAN

I believe Jamie would be pleased to know his mantle of inspiration and example is being taken up by more than one who came into the kingdom because of the words he wrote. Writers like Jamie are few. Having a friend like Jamie is a gift from God.

—**DAN MALACHUK**, PUBLISHER

Jamie was a prophet with a pen. He was the kind of person who would ask the Lord questions and refuse to accept canned answers. We needed him, and we will need others like him.

—**BOB MUMFORD**, BIBLE TEACHER

The ministry of Jamie was the epitome of the "ministry of reconciliation" in the body of Christ. He held the esteem of conservative, evangelical circles. He was universally received by the Pentecostal church. He challenged and helped direct the growth of charismatics, and he won the confidence of institutionally minded Christians across the world.

—**TOMMY TYSON**, EVANGELIST

Jamie never failed to write and speak with great humor or poignancy—but the startling constant was his clarity. You might be chuckling or crying, but you always understood the point he was making. He saw God everywhere and in everything, and that delighted him. He just had to tell stories about it.

—**BOB SLOSSER**, JOURNALIST

Jamie was a gifted man with a lot of energy. His days were packed with kingdom activity. What impressed me most, however, was his humble transparency. He didn't pretend to have all the answers, and he was open about his faults.

—**MARK BUCKLEY**, PASTOR

A
SPIRIT-LED
LIFE

A
SPIRIT-LED
LIFE

JAMIE BUCKINGHAM

BL BRIDGE
LOGOS

Newberry, FL 32669

Bridge-Logos
Newberry, FL 32669

A Spirit-Led Life:
My Personal Journey to Life in the Spirit
by Jamie Buckingham
Edited for print by Bruce and Michele Buckingham

Risky Living Ministries is dedicated to preserving the teachings and life works of Jamie Buckingham.

www.RLMin.com
www.JamieBuckinghamMinistries.com

Printed in the United States of America.

Library of Congress Catalog Card Number: 2022937661

International Standard Book Number: 978-1-61036-276-4

Cover/Interior design by Kent Jensen | knail.com

Cover photo of Jamie Buckingham by Bruce Buckingham

BP 08/2022

TABLE OF CONTENTS

FOREWORD

This small but impacting book is the kind that only Jamie Buckingham could have given rise to.

I have been amazed for years now as to how timeless Jamie Buckingham's teachings and insights are. I remember the first time I heard Jamie speak about the Spirit. It caught me totally off guard. His insights were alive, free from any pigeon-holed theological angles. They were just plain true.

If you have never heard or read anything by Jamie, start with this book. You will feel like you have finally come home after a twenty-year journey. That is what I tell those who are just becoming acquainted with his teaching: it is like coming home for Christmas after a long absence.

I thank Bruce, Jamie's eldest son, for the amazing sacrifice he has made in getting Jamie's materials out onto living room tables again. Bruce is an awful lot like his dad—maybe as much so as anyone I have known. Every single project he has done over the last few years has been focused, true to what I remember hearing Jamie teach live, and demonstrates Jamie's take-no-prisoners approach toward stale religion—as well as his non-judgmental compassion toward the rest of us, wherever we are on our spiritual journey.

Doug Murren
Author, *The Baby Boomerang*
Founder/Director, The Murren Group
Wenatchee, Washington

INTRODUCTION

My father, Jamie Buckingham, always spoke and wrote with great personal transparency. When teaching about God, Jesus, and the Spirit-filled life—whether from the platform in the church he pastored in Melbourne, Florida, or from the stage at some far-away conference attended by thousands—his own life was always an open book.

To listen to my dad, to read his books, was to know him. He never held back. He was determined to be honest and authentic before the Lord and before others. As a result, over his 30-plus years of ministry, he revealed a lot about himself—about his life, about his relationship with God, about his personal spiritual journey. And he did so with extraordinary grace, humility, and self-deprecating humor.

He never wrote an actual autobiography. But, as it turns out, he did speak one.

A Spirit-Led Life is adapted from a series of five messages Dad preached in April 1990 to Graceland Baptist Church in New Albany, Indiana. I discovered this series in my quest to collect as many of his recorded teachings as possible after his death in February 1992. (I now have over 900 cassette tapes that I'm slowly but steadily digitizing and adding to the Jamie Buckingham Ministries website.) These five messages—for our purposes here, five chapters—tell his story. Not in perfectly linear fashion, and not without numerous teaching stops, but it's all there: the good, the bad, the ugly, the joyful, the supernatural, the glorious.

What is also there is a challenge: will you and I step out, take a risk, and open ourselves to the fullness of the Holy Spirit, which God has prepared for us in Christ Jesus? That's what Dad did, in his own imperfectly perfect way. He learned—sometimes slowly and painfully, sometimes instantly and joyfully—how to live a Spirit-led life and, in the process, fulfill his God-given dreams.

I believe God wants all His children to dream big, God-sized dreams; to take risks; to step out in faith; to be filled with His Holy Spirit to follow Him, wherever He leads. If that's what you believe, too—or if you want to believe it—please turn the page. Read my father's story. Then, as you are filled and led by the Holy Spirit, go forth and write your own.

Bruce Buckingham
President, Risky Living Ministries
Palm Bay, Florida

CHAPTER 1

HOW DREAMS COME TRUE

It was five years ago when your pastor and I first talked about my coming to Graceland Baptist Church here in New Albany, Indiana. It has taken that long to work out the details. I don't know if a specific proposal needed to be submitted to a committee or not. I know something of Baptist committees and how they work. But it has finally come to pass, and I am honored—really overjoyed—to be here.

My wife, Jackie, spoke to me this morning as I was preparing my message. She reminded me that we've waited a long time for this—and by "this" she means getting back into the pulpit of a Baptist church.

I've been *persona non grata* in a lot of Baptist churches for reasons you'll find out soon enough. After growing up as a Southern Baptist and pastoring in Southern Baptist churches for years, I went through the traumatic experience of having the Florida Baptist Convention invite our entire church to *not* be a

Baptist church anymore. It was hard to take at first. We were—I was—following the leading of the Holy Spirit, and apparently that rubbed some of the convention leaders the wrong way. So, we were excommunicated.

Going through that experience—and now, after all these years, watching God restore those relationships—has been wonderful. And there is more restoration coming, because some of those who wanted so desperately to have us ushered out have now had their own fresh encounter with the Holy Spirit. There is a new breeze blowing throughout the entire kingdom of God.

Just last month I sat down with James Robison. James is a Southern Baptist evangelist based out of Fort Worth, Texas. He has been used by God all across the world. Recently he asked me and five others to serve on what he calls the World Council of Evangelism. This is actually a personal advisory board for his ministry—a Southern Baptist ministry.

We had our first meeting last month in Phoenix. I was with Richard Jackson and John Morgan, who are pastors of two of the largest Southern Baptist churches in the convention. One is in Phoenix and the other is in Houston. Also attending was Tommy Barnett, pastor of the very large Phoenix First Assembly in Phoenix, Arizona [renamed Dream Center Church]. Also, there was my good friend Jack Hayford from The Church on the Way in Van Nuys, California. That's a Foursquare church. So, there were two Pentecostals, two Southern Baptists, and me—a maverick, a charismatic, an independent. I'm there, a non-denominationalist, in the midst of all these great men of God coming together in unity for the primary purpose of praying for world evangelism, believing that this is of primary importance to God in this decade.

We joined together in unity, laying aside our doctrinal differences—and there are some great differences. But we laid those differences aside in order to focus on one particular issue: trusting God to bless these efforts in world evangelism. And I am so grateful for that.

I really do believe there is a new wind blowing. That is the sound we hear "in the tops of the mulberry trees," as the King James Version states in 2 Samuel 5:24:

> As soon as you hear the sound of marching in the tops of the balsam [mulberry] trees, move quickly, because that will mean the Lord has gone out in front of you to strike the Philistine army.

It is the sound of victory. God is going forth throughout this nation. He is moving in the hearts of men and women—His people—in every corner of the church.

The kingdom of God has been shaken over the last several years, as some high-profile Christian leaders have had their personal troubles made public. It's been ugly. And some denominations, including the Southern Baptists, have been rattled all the way down to the roots with their own internal struggles.

But God is beginning to blow His fresh breath into these and other situations, saying, "It's time to lay aside divisive things and move into the deeper matters of what the kingdom of God is all about."

So that's why I am so glad we are going to be spending a few days together. I'm looking forward to it. It's going to be a good time for all of us.

I am so grateful for the work God has done and continues to do. It's been interesting to see how many of the things that have gone on here are so much like what my church in Melbourne, Florida, experienced back in the late 1960's and early 1970's.

I'm a writer. I'm an editor. I'm a storyteller. I'm also the pastor of a church. If I'd focus all my time on any one of those positions, I could probably feel more successful. But I don't give full time to any one role, and as a result sometimes everything feels half-done. But I am following the Spirit of God, and that means moving when and where He moves me.

God spoke to me very specifically when I accepted your pastor's invitation to come here. I sensed Him saying, "Speak to the hearts of the people, because I have a message from My heart to their hearts."

That message is this: God has placed inside each one of us—deep down inside—a spiritual dream. It is a part of us. It is what the Creator built into each one of us when He formed us. It's part of the image of God He purposefully placed inside our hearts. It's that which God has breathed into us—a little bit of Himself. And it's that part which is calling us unto Him.

There is inside of me, and there is inside of you, a longing to be like God, to please Him, to reflect Him. We want to be like Jesus. We want to have the same power and authority and character He had when He was walking on this earth. As followers of Christ, we really want that. We can deny it, but the truth is that each one of us has this longing, this dream.

At the same time, many of us don't seem to want it badly enough to do anything about it. Perhaps we are satisfied to just yearn for it, to dream about it, to wish we were different. We want it, yet we don't want it.

Jesus came to set us free so that we can be like Him. And yet, there's a conflict going on inside us. We say we want to be like Christ; but at the same time, we really like doing things our own way. The sacrificial aspect of knowing Him—the willingness to pay a price to be like Jesus—is the thing that is constantly ripping and tearing at us.

Let's keep all this in mind as we look at Psalm 37:3-4. It's a passage many of you are familiar with. Verse 3 says:

> Trust in the Lord and do good; dwell in the land and enjoy safe pasture.

As believers, we know that's possible. We know it's possible to be secure in a world that is insecure. We know it's possible to be safe in a world that is unsafe. We know it's possible to prosper in a world that is not prosperous, to be healthy in a world that's unhealthy, to live in a world that is dying. The question is, how badly do we want it?

The big problem we seem to have is found in verse 4:

> Delight yourself in the Lord and He will give you the desires of your heart.

As we grow older and walk a little bit longer with the Lord, I think we begin to recognize that the desires of our heart are rarely the desires of God's heart. And yet that is what we need. We need to have the desires of our heart transformed, so that our desires are in line with His desires. When that occurs, God promises to give us what He wants—and, amazingly, it will be what we want, too.

When we desire the same things that God wants for us, we can have those desires by simply asking Him for them.

But how do His desires become our desires? How do we get to that place? Maybe you don't really want to know how to get there. Maybe you think the journey will be too hard, or too painful, or too discouraging. Maybe the real question we need to answer is, will it be worth it?

I'm going share a little bit of my personal testimony this morning, and it speaks to the question of how we get there—how our desires can turn into God's desires—and why it's worth it. By the time I finish, you may say, "I wish he hadn't said all that stuff." But come back tonight, because we are going talk about it further.

As I said, I'm an editor, a writer, so I deal in chapters. Tonight, I am going to give you Chapter 2. Be sure and come back for it. But this morning I'm going give you Chapter 1 and talk about this concept of how our dreams can come true. Then, later, we will talk about the marvelous experience called being filled, or baptized, in the Holy Spirit.

I will tell you what the Scriptures have to say and what I've experienced personally. I will tell you about the things I have witnessed and how they set the stage for everything else that has happened in my Spirit-led walk with the Lord.

If we're going to be like Jesus, then we have to start by being baptized in the Holy Spirit. You simply can't be like Jesus by just reading the Bible or attending church services or being a good person. Something has got to happen on the inside. Change must come from within. It can't come from without. Later, in the sessions to follow, we'll get into this idea more.

I will also talk to you about miracles and how you, too, can be a miracle worker. Now if you are not interested in miracles, feel free to stay away. In fact, it will probably be a good thing for you to *not* get involved. But if, in your heart, you really are interested in the working of God and the movement of the Holy Spirit—if there is a curiosity within you—then, by all means, be here.

If you are wondering, "Is it possible for me to experience such things?" I'm here to tell you this week that, yes, it is possible for you. It is possible for each one of you.

God's power is available to you. It's providential that you have it. I think you are preordained for it, frankly. And there are some very simple things you can do that will open wonderful new doors of blessing, power, and intimacy with Christ, as you move forward in your walk with Him.

THE DARK PIT

When I go out to conduct an interview for a story, I take my recorder and my notebook, and I sit down with the person. It may be someone who's had an interesting experience in life. Maybe it's an athlete. Maybe it's a politician. Maybe it's a businessman. Maybe it's a housewife. Maybe it's a preacher or a missionary. Everybody's got a story. I'm not talking about a recounting of all the days of a person's life, but rather one big, defining, life-changing story that begs to be told. When I go out, I look for that story. That's what writers do—they question and probe until they discover what the story is.

When I am looking for that one big, defining story in a person's life, I go to the place any good writer or journalist knows to look first—the place where he or she always starts. I know if I can get to that one place, the big story will begin to emerge.

That place is what writers call "the dark pit" in a person's life.

Everybody has a dark pit. The dark pit is that time when something happened, and you felt as if all the lights went out in your life. It's that time when your dreams were dashed, when all

7

your hopes and ambitions were rubbed out. It's that time when everything you had planned for yourself was taken away—blown out like a candle in a hurricane.

Every one of us has had at least one dark pit experience. And if you haven't yet, you will. It seems common to all mankind. You planned for a marriage; it dissolved. You planned for a child; he died. You planned to make money; you wound up broke. You planned to be free; you got thrown in prison.

Everything was going along just fine, then suddenly you were betrayed. Fired. Sidelined by illness. Punched in the gut by a circumstance you never saw coming.

I know I can get to the heart of somebody's story if I can get them to start talking about their dark pit experience—how it happened, what took place. *Then* I know I have a story. Everybody is interested in hearing about the dark pits in the lives of other people, because they know they have one, too. Saint John of the Cross, the Roman Catholic scholar and mystic, calls this pit "the dark night of the soul." If you haven't experienced one yet, hang on! And if you have been through one already, hang on, because there may be another one coming. We all love the mountaintop experiences of life. But life is also made up of experiences in the valley—dark pit experiences.

Now, there are those who say that once you become a Christian, all you do is bounce on a Jesus pogo stick from mountaintop to mountaintop to mountaintop. But that just ain't so. About every third mountain top, you miss the mountain and go off the cliff. I'm not telling you this to discourage you. I'm telling you this simply because this is the way life is made, and you need to know it. But it's in the valley experiences that marvelous things happen. And if you understand that God is the

God of valleys as well as the God of mountaintops, then you will praise Him no matter what your circumstances are.

Twenty-five years ago, I went through my own dark pit experience.

You see, I grew up in a Christian home. Well, let me rephrase that: I grew up in a church-going home. There is a difference. My mother and father were both good church members. My dad taught a men's Bible class at the Methodist church. My mother was active in the Christian church. As a family, we compromised and joined a community church in our hometown of Vero Beach, Florida, that didn't believe in any denominational doctrines in particular, but rather everything in general.

We were basically fundamentalists. We had very high and noble moral standards in our house. I remember the time my mother cancelled the Sunday newspaper because, as she said, "We are going to keep the Sabbath." My siblings and I could no longer read the Sunday comics. I still remember my argument with her. I explained that Sunday is not the Sabbath; Saturday is the Sabbath. So she cancelled the Saturday paper, too.

For years we lived as if maintaining a high moral code and trying to live up to impossible standards were the equivalent of being Christian. Then one day, after I went off to college, my parents met Jesus Christ on a personal, intimate level. They invited Him into their hearts and, in the process, came out of their own dark pit.

My father and mother had moved to Florida right after World War II. My mom was from Winchester, Kentucky; my dad was from the little town of Morristown, Indiana, outside Indianapolis. It's interesting that I'm here this week, not too far from both of their hometowns.

After my parents had their personal experience with Jesus, they decided to join the Southern Baptist church. I had already joined the Baptist church for a good spiritual reason: it was where my girlfriend went.

My decision paid off, too. I married her, and she has stuck with me ever since. But my folks joined the Baptist church because it was a Bible-teaching, Bible-believing church. They became hungry for the Word of God and interested in the Bible in a whole new way. Now the Word was personal to them, not just academic.

Then, in my senior year in college, I had my own experience with Jesus Christ and gave my life to Him. It was my first real, personal acquaintance with the Lord, and it happened at Schroon Lake, New York, under the ministry of Jack Wyrtzen, the old fundamentalist radio preacher.

As a result, after graduation, I decided to go to Southwestern Baptist Theological Seminary in Ft. Worth, Texas, to train to become a pastor. Four years later, I got my first pastorate at a large Southern Baptist church in Greenwood, South Carolina. I moved to Greenwood with my wife, Jackie, and our young son, Bruce. During the eight years we were in Greenwood, our family of three grew to a family of seven. By all appearances, we were a perfect Southern Baptist ministry family.

Then, suddenly, everything changed. I was abruptly fired, because I had developed a relationship with another woman in the church.

That was back long before it was popular to have an affair. Now, it seems, everybody is doing it. Well, not everybody! I don't mean that. But back then, it was never talked about, and no one knew how to handle it. So, they just cut your throat and threw you out in the woods. And that's what happened to me—or, at least, that's what it felt like.

There I was, wandering around aimlessly with my wife and five kids, because the church had decided to get rid of me. At first, I couldn't wrap my mind around it. As a church, we had a lot of good things going. We were a big Baptist congregation. We had good programs, and a lot of folks were involved. I was a popular young pastor. But soon I realized that what happened wasn't the church's fault. It was my fault. I began to understand, as I lay there bleeding, that the reason all this was happening to me was *me*.

I was empty.

It's a terrible thing to have the call of God and not the power of God. It's a terrible thing to try to do God's work without His presence in your life.

That's what I had done for eight years. For eight years in that church, I had preached other people's sermons. And I was good at it. I could memorize a Herschel Hobbs sermon, a Charles Allen sermon—all the great pulpiteers. I got their books, and I memorized their sermons. It would all come back to me in the pulpit, and I could preach a sermon as though it were mine. Everybody thought it was great—that I was great. But I was hollow. Empty. There was nothing real on the inside to reinforce what I was saying on the outside.

Then there was an enticement. It came out of a friendly relationship, the kind all pastors have. It moved in on me, and before I knew it, I was into a situation that I shouldn't have been into. In hindsight, I know I should have run, but I didn't know how to get out of it. No, that's not true. I didn't *want* to get out of it, because I thought it was filling an emptiness inside of me that—I discovered much later—could only be filled by the Holy Spirit.

So, we left South Carolina. I took my wife and five children, and I began pastoring a tiny little Baptist church in Melbourne, Florida. Then, 15 months later, I was thrown out of that church, too, because I hadn't told them why I had been fired from the first church. If I'd told them, they never would have hired me. I didn't lie to them, I just didn't tell the whole truth—which is almost worse than a lie.

Some in the congregation had gotten suspicious. They'd hired a private investigator, and he'd told them the entire story of why I was fired in Greenwood. I stood up one Sunday morning to preach, and there was a petition on the podium, signed by two-thirds of the congregation—the very people sitting in the pews—asking me to resign. I don't know how I did it, but I preached anyway. The next Sunday, somebody else was preaching.

I had figured that, sooner or later, it would all come out. It would all come crashing down on me again. And sure enough, it did. Suddenly I was in that black pit again. Everything was gone. There was no hope for me and my family. I had two strikes against me now. I was out. Finished. I had no idea what God wanted of me or for me.

GOD'S PLAN

In the middle of all of that horrible turmoil—when I thought my life was over, when I thought everything had come to a close—something amazing happened. A bush caught fire.

I picked up a copy of a little interfaith magazine called *Guideposts*. I knew nothing about it. All I saw was a tiny publication filled with nice little stories. Because it was "interfaith," it had stories about Jews and Catholics and Mormons and Christians. I thought that everybody who wasn't a Baptist was either a Jew, a Catholic, a Mormon or a non-Christian. I didn't know very much. I didn't know very much about the kingdom of God. I didn't know how broad God's kingdom is. I didn't occur to me there might be Christians who weren't Baptist.

I didn't know that God was working in all sectors of His kingdom. I thought He was only working in the tiny little sector of Christianity that I was involved with. That's all. I didn't know how big He is.

Anyway, I got hold of this little magazine and flipped through it, because I didn't have anything else to do. I didn't have to prepare sermons anymore, because I didn't have a pulpit. I'd been cast out of everything familiar, and all my lights had gone out. But then I saw an ad for a writers contest. "Send in a manuscript," it said. "If your manuscript is one of those we choose, we'll pay your expenses to come to a week-long writers' conference in New York, sponsored by the magazine. We'll help you learn how to write."

So, I decided to send in a manuscript. After all, I didn't have a job. Nobody wanted me. I was *persona non grata* everywhere I went. But I did know how to write. I'd written 10 years' worth of sermons—even if nobody was interested in hearing me preach them anymore.

Since I had nothing but time, I sat down at a typewriter, and I followed the instructions explicitly: first-person story, 750 words, double-spaced. I did all that, put the manuscript in an envelope, and dropped it in the mail.

And then I got a telegram back from the publishers.

"We received over 5,000 manuscripts, and we chose 20 of them," they wrote. "Yours is one of the 20. We're sending you a plane ticket, and you're flying up to New York City. You are going to meet for a week at a retreat center on Long Island Sound with the editors of *Guideposts Magazine*."

I didn't know what to think. All I knew was that my heart had been crushed, and everything I had dreamed of and hoped for was gone. I didn't know God was going to take everything that had happened in the past and mold it into something magnificent for the future. I didn't have faith for that. I didn't believe that. Even as a pastor, I didn't know enough about God to know that He would do that.

But when you're in a black pit, it really doesn't make any difference what you believe about God, because regardless of what you believe or think, He still has a plan and purpose for you. It doesn't make any difference how much you know about God, as long as you allow Him to know something about you. It's not about what you do or believe, anyway. It's about God's grace and God's mercy.

In those times when all the lights went out in my life, God always had something better planned for me. He always had a burning bush waiting out there on a mountainside for me, just as He did for Moses.

Back then I didn't know much about burning bushes. I'd read the story in Exodus 3, but I didn't really know anything about them firsthand. Since then, however, I've discovered some things about burning bushes.

For example, you can't see their light until all the other lights go out in your life. As long as there is something burning brightly in your life, you will not see what God has lit for you along the way. As long as you have other voices speaking into your life, you will not hear the voice of God, because those other voices will drown it out. It's only when all the other voices are quieted and all the other lights are out that you can really hear God, that you can really see Him.

Think about Moses. After 40 years of tending sheep on the same mountainside, he suddenly notices an odd sight. A bush is burning, but it is not being consumed by the flames. I can hear Moses saying to himself, "Well, I don't have anything else to do. My life is pretty empty, compared to what it used to be. All I'm doing now is minding these stupid sheep. I think I'll mosey over there and see what's going on."

Now, I have my own theory about the burning bush. I believe that bush had been burning for a long time. I think Moses had gone back and forth along that same mountain path for decades. It just took him all that time to finally pay attention to what God wanted to say to him.

I don't think God only speaks to you once. I think God has been speaking to you all along. I don't think God lets His bush burn once, and if you fail to notice it and go see it, you'll miss it forever. I think He lets it burn continuously until you turn aside and approach it.

Sometimes God has to bring you to a place where all hope is gone. In Moses' case, all the lights of Egypt have finally gone out. All the voices of Egypt have finally stilled. That's when he sees the fire out of the corner of his eye and says, "I think I'll turn aside and see what's going on over there." And the moment he does, there is a big voice that speaks to him saying, "I am who I am." Then He adds, "Moses, I have a job for you."

In my case, I got a telegram that said, "Jamie, come to New York." So, I turned toward the burning bush and got on a plane.

I'd never been to New York City. I'm a Southern boy from a small town. Except for the one time I went to Schroon Lake in upstate New York, I'd never been further north than North Carolina. The furthest west I'd been was Texas, when I went to seminary. Before that, I once visited Nashville, Tennessee. For a Southern Baptist, that was like going to Mecca, or the Vatican. I thought, "Praise Nashville from which all blessings flow." A small-town Baptist boy visiting Nashville? Wow!

I didn't know there was a world that existed outside those parameters—and suddenly I was in it. I got off the plane in New York City that Sunday afternoon, where I was met by someone who put me in a van and drove me up to a beautiful retreat center on Long Island Sound. Soon I was with 20 other people I'd never met before. I had no idea who they were. They had come in from all around the nation, because they, too, had submitted a manuscript and had been judged as very good—or potentially very good—writers. And there I was in the midst of them, meeting with the staff of *Guideposts Magazine*.

That Sunday evening after dinner, about 30 of us sat down in big sofas and easy chairs in the living room of a huge stone mansion. It was late October, and a fire was in the fireplace. Walnut-paneled walls, tall bookcases, heavy draperies on the windows—you can picture the scene.

Old Dr. Norman Vincent Peale, founder of *Guideposts Magazine*, was there. I knew nothing about him except that he was pastor of Marble Collegiate Church in New York City and a rank liberal. And I thought, "What in the world am I doing in the room with this old liberal theologian?" As far as I knew, Dr. Peale believed everything and didn't believe anything. That was the rumor I had heard.

And then the other people in the room—who were they? Catherine Marshall, the author of the bestselling novel *Christy*, was there, and her husband, Len LeSourd, who was the executive editor of *Guideposts* at the time. John Sherrill was there. I knew John had written a couple of books, but I didn't know much about them. I'd heard of one: *The Cross and the Switchblade*, about a Pentecostal preacher named David Wilkerson in New York City. Another was called *I Speak with Other Tongues*. I knew nothing about that one.

After we all settled in, old Dr. Peale said, "Well, it's a special night. Each one of you has been chosen to be here. We're going to go around the room and let each of you introduce yourselves. Tell us who you are, because we're going to spend the next week together, and we want to know more about you and how you got started as a writer."

I was sitting over to one side, and one by one everyone started introducing themselves. All these writers, flown to New York at the expense of *Guideposts*—I couldn't take it. These were successful people—I mean, really successful people. The editor of the Des Moines newspaper was sitting there. Another man who had already written 19 books was next to him. There was a woman who had written 95 magazine articles, and another lady who was the editor of the *Catholic Register*. Everyone was from a different denominational background. The editor of the Marriott Hotels newsletter was there. He said he was a Mormon. (I found out later he was really an agnostic. He didn't like Mormons, and he didn't like Christians. He was a crusty old guy.) And there were others: a Roman Catholic, a Presbyterian, a Methodist.

Then there was me.

I hadn't written anything except all those sermons nobody wanted anymore, and it was almost my turn to introduce myself. I watched as, one by one, each person took their turn to talk about their many accomplishments. I didn't have anything comparable to brag about. What could I say? "Hi, I'm Jamie Buckingham. I live down in Florida, and I have been thrown out of two Baptist churches. Why? I can't tell you, because it would be too embarrassing"?

It's terrible to be in a place where you can't be honest, because you're such a failure. I mean, you can't even fake it. There's nothing to fake.

As it was coming up on my turn, I did the only thing I could think to do. I turned and whispered to the person next to me, "I've got to go to the bathroom." Then I stood up and walked out of the room.

I waited outside the door until the introductions passed my empty chair, like the wave at a baseball game. Then I sneaked back in and took my seat again. They never did call on me. I didn't have anything to say, and I didn't want to say anything. I didn't want them to know who I was.

When it was all over, Dr. Peale—who I realize now was one of God's prophets—spoke. Bless his heart. To this day I believe he was looking straight at me when he said, "Tonight is the first day of the rest of your life. God has marvelous, wonderful things for you. And you will see these magnificent things take place, because you are here tonight."

In that moment, the light that had been blown out by sin and circumstances came back on again. Sitting there in that room, I felt it flicker back into existence in my heart.

That night I went up to my tiny cubicle that had just enough room for a single bed and a chest of drawers. I lay in that bed all night long listening to the music—the music that was all in my head.

Everybody else had gone to sleep. But for the first time in years, I heard the joyous sounds of music again. A light was burning, and it kept me awake all night long.

I got up early the next morning, before dawn, and walked alone along the jetties on Long Island Sound. I looked down the Sound towards Manhattan, and I could see the tall buildings of the city beginning to poke up out of the early morning mist. The sun was just catching the tops of them as it came up across Staten Island.

As I sat down on the rocks and watched the sun rise, one of the young ladies in our group, a Catholic writer from Seattle, came out and sat down beside me.

I'd never sat beside a Catholic before. My mother told me to never date Catholic girls—if I did, she said, a mean priest might come after me. So, I stayed away from them. But now this Catholic woman was sitting beside me. She reached over, took my hand, and said, "I think God sent me out here to pray with you." She didn't know who I was. She didn't know anything about me. She'd only seen me the night before.

"I think God wants me to pray with you," she said again. And she began to pray.

I didn't know Catholics knew how to pray. I thought they just counted those funny little beads. But she prayed with me, and my world got a million times bigger. Suddenly I saw all of God's people that I'd never known were God's people being used by the Holy Spirit in ways I knew nothing about. God was saying to me, "Jamie, I'm going to show you something special."

Before the week was out, a man in the jewelry business in Plainfield, New Jersey, contacted John Sherrill, the writer of *The Cross and the Switchblade*. This jewelry dealer—a Russian

Pentecostal named Dan Malchuk—said, "I believe God wants me to go into the publishing business, and I have signed up a Puerto Rican boy by the name of Nicky Cruz as the subject of my first book to be released."

Of course, John Sherrill knew Nicky Cruz. Nicky is the former New York City street gang member who was featured in Sherrill's best-selling book, *The Cross and the Switchblade*.

Now Malachuk wanted John to write the sequel. He was the obvious choice. John's initial response was no, but he agreed to pray about it. Later that evening, he called Dan Malachuk back and said, "I still don't think I am the right person to write your book. I believe God wants somebody else to do it, and that fellow is here at this conference. I'm going to put you in touch with him."

The next day I got a call from publisher Dan Malachuk, and before the week was out, I had signed a contract to write a book.

I didn't know anything about books or contracts. And yet I signed a contract to write a book that we later titled *Run Baby Run*. I finished it in five months, and it sold over two million copies before the end of the year. To date it has sold more than nine million copies and has been translated into 28 different languages. It was my first book. And suddenly I realized God is a big, big God.

If God knows your name—and He does—that's all that really counts. It is God who places the dreams in your heart. I didn't even know I had a dream to be a writer or an editor or a publisher. I didn't think I had a dream for anything except climbing up some ecclesiastical ladder in the Southern Baptist Church. That's all I knew.

But God said, "I've got something so much bigger for you, if you'll just let Me take control. It won't look like what you thought it would look like. It will look like Me instead."

TURNING LOOSE

I want to encourage you today. I want to encourage you to be willing to turn loose in the tough times. You have probably heard the saying, "Let go and let God." Stop trying to hang on to that dream that is in your heart. If you'll let go of your dream, even if it's been given to you by prophetic word, God will take it, and He will do something with it.

You say, "But God promised." Yes, God has promised. But let go even of God's promises and hold fast instead to the Promiser. Then let Him do something special in your life.

I know where you are. I've walked there before. I've lived there before. My kids are living there now. I'm struggling with all five of them as they struggle to make their own way. Each one of them has a dream. But I know the principles that have applied to my life apply to their lives, also, and they apply to yours. Not until you let go of your dreams will they ever become reality.

I have been reading former President Richard Nixon's book called *In the Arena*. At one time Nixon was the world's most powerful and respected leader. He writes about what he has learned primarily from failure—the failure of the Watergate scandal in particular. I'm intrigued with what he has to say.

Last Thursday night, I flew out to Tulsa, Oklahoma. I spoke at the annual banquet for the Honors Society at Oral Roberts University. The Honors Society is the Phi Beta Kappa organization on that campus. In order to belong, you have to have a grade point average of 3.8 or better out of a possible 4.0 for four years.

It's fun to speak to people who are really smart. Most of the people I speak to have about the same intelligence I do. So, this was really fun and stimulating, speaking to people who are smarter than I am. And these folks *are* smarter than me. They are so smart that they laughed before I got to my punch line. I was just getting started on my funny story, and they were nine steps ahead of me. They had already figured out where I was going and were laughing before I had finished the joke.

It was great. I didn't even have to finish a sentence. They finished it for me. I only had to get it started then move on to the next sentence.

But I did chide them. And the reason I chided them was because, as I told them, "None of you are failures. You can't fail even one course in college and get into the honors society. One failure, and you're disqualified.

"I applaud your success," I continued. "I applaud that you strive for excellence. I think it's mandatory. I do it myself. I'm a writer, and that means I work over words and punctuation, sentences and ideas. I write and I rewrite, and I rewrite, and I rewrite, until what I've written is excellent. And even then, I know it can be improved."

Frankly, I've never read anything that couldn't be improved by an editor or another rewrite—except the Bible, of course. And I have problems with the first chapter of Ephesians sometimes.

But at the same time, the striving for excellence and the mastering of success is not where life is. That was my point to the Phi Beta Kappas. Life is in the real world. And in the real world, people fail. In the real world, you don't get a hit every time you come up to bat. A lot of times you strike out. In fact, in major league baseball, you're a success if you can get a hit one out of four times at the plate. Twenty-five percent, and you're a success!

In the real world, failure is where it's at. In fact, failure is not only your greatest teacher; failure is your *only* teacher. You don't learn from success. The only one you learn from is Professor Failure. He's the only one who teaches you. As long as you're succeeding, there are no lessons to be learned. The only time you learn is when you've been crushed by life, and failure is yours.

Richard Nixon said he learned three things from his Watergate failure. Remember how he was disgraced and forced to resign as President of the United States, before he could be impeached? He was the most hated, most maligned man in the world at that time. You couldn't turn on a late-night comedy TV show without hearing somebody making fun of Richard Nixon.

But through that experience, Nixon said he learned, first of all, that failure or defeat is never fatal unless you give up. Second, he learned that failure or defeat puts your weaknesses in perspective and allows you to develop a stronger immune system, so you can handle the next failure that's coming down the road. You'll never be able to handle the next one unless you learn how to handle this one. And third, Nixon learned that you never know how strong you can be when things go smoothly; you only tap into God's power when you're forced to cope with adversity.

Shortly after Nixon resigned in disgrace, he said his body stopped functioning. He said he'd made it through all the stress and trauma of being President of the United States; then when he resigned and stepped out of office, everything in him just stopped working. Previously he'd had blood clots in his leg; in fact, he almost lost his leg to thrombophlebitis. When he stepped down, though, the blood clots formed in his stomach, and he was rushed into emergency surgery. They thought he was going to die. In the operating room, his blood pressure dropped to fifty over zero. His pulse was undetectable. The doctors resuscitated him there on the operating table.

After he was revived and the surgery was done, he was moved to the recovery room. He told his wife, Pat, "I'm finished. It's over. Life is over."

He said, "I understand now how Lyndon [Johnson] died so soon after he left the presidency. That's where I am now. I don't want to live anymore. I have nothing. I'm finished. I've lost my will to live."

Years later, writing his memoirs, Nixon said two things pulled him through that tough time, and I find them very interesting.

The first thing happened in his hospital room, which was on the ninth floor. He'd had all the drapes pulled, and it was dark. He didn't want to live. He had just told his wife that he wanted to die. He had asked her to leave him alone, pull the plugs out, and let him die.

Suddenly a nurse rushed in and pulled open the drapes. She said, "Mr. President, quick, look out the window!"

Nixon was attached to all kinds of wires and tubes and had to strain his neck to look in her direction. That's when he saw a little airplane flying by the ninth-floor window. It was a two-winged biplane pulling a banner behind it. And the banner said, "God loves you, Richard Nixon, and so do we."

Later Nixon learned it was Billy Graham's wife, Ruth, who had arranged for that airplane to fly back and forth in front of his hospital window. Now, that's better than sending flowers!

Nixon said the second thing that pulled him through and kept him going was a little note that had been handed to him by Clare Boothe Luce, the daughter of the founder of the Time/Life organization.

She was sitting beside him in a meeting one day after the Watergate scandal had broken, and there was serious talk in Washington of impeachment. She was a member of the Foreign Intelligence Advisory Board. It was just three days before he resigned. And at this meeting she handed Nixon a note. He folded it and put it in his pocket, not reading it at the time. It wasn't until he got back to the White House that night and was considering again that option of resigning that he opened the note and looked at it.

It was a quote from Andrew Barton, a Scottish sailor in the early 1500's. After a fierce battle, Barton said, "I am hurt but I am not slain. I'll lay me down and bleed awhile. Then I'll rise and fight again."

That's what took place on Good Friday, when the lights of the world went out and cruel men nailed the Son of God to a cross. They blew out the candle of world hope, and God died on the cross. He was buried in a grave, and the forces of hell rejoiced.

Three days later, true to the promise of the Scriptures, the Holy Spirit came into that tomb and filled the dead body of the Son of God with life. The grave exploded in power, and the light of the world went back on again.

And that light still shines today as brightly as ever. He lives! And not only does He live, but He is still giving life.

The Jews have a word for it: *chaim*. Life. And I believe that Jesus is still toasting all the people of the world with *L'chaim*. To life! "I have come to you," Jesus said, "that you might have life.

And not only that you might have life, but you might have it more abundantly."

Now you will not get *chaim* until you die. You will not get life unless you first go to the cross. For without the cross, there can be no resurrection. There must first be a cross.

Jesus is alive today and He is giving life. I stand here before you this morning, not preaching a sermon. I *am* a sermon. I stand before you as a testimony of what God does when the Holy Spirit moves upon someone who has no place to go but up.

I bring you today a message of hope. When the lights go out in your life and you are in the dark pit, have hope! God has something good for you. This really can be the first day of the rest of your life, if you will turn loose and let God take control.

Father, in Jesus' name, I want to thank You for Your goodness and Your graciousness. I want to thank You that You don't kick us when we're down. That You don't batter us like other people batter us. That You don't continually point out our sins like others do. But rather, You light the candle of hope again in our lives. And You let the face of Jesus shine before us all night long. I pray, Lord, that You light that candle again in the hearts and minds and lives of Your people. Amen.

CHAPTER 2

THE BAPTISM OF THE HOLY SPIRIT

I appreciate having grandchildren. Most grandparents have grandkids who only come to visit. All of mine happen to live with me, along with all of my adult children, in our little community in the Florida countryside.

Somebody told me that when your kids grow up and go off to school, that's the beginning of a new life. For me it's not the beginning of a new life; it's an extension of the old life—only much more expensive. Not only did my kids grow up and get married, but they came back home—and they're all poor.

All five of our children went off to college. Some of them found spouses and brought them back home. My eldest son, Bruce, had to move to Washington, D.C., for a few years to find his beautiful wife, Michele.

A while back we bought 20 acres of land on the outskirts of the little town of Palm Bay, Florida, out amongst the tall pine trees. We offered each child an acre of land so they would come back and build their houses near my house. It's like a Bedouin camp now, with the patriarch in his tent and all these other little tents around it. And the couples in those tents have spawned many times, with no end in sight.

So, I have all these little people in and out of the house all the time. Actually, I currently have four generations living inside my house. Jackie's mother, Daisy, who is 82, has Parkinson's disease. Sometimes she does great; other times she doesn't get out of bed. She's with us. And then my youngest son, Tim, his wife, Kathy, and his three little ones are with us while he is remodeling a house we moved from down the street and set up on the backside of our 20 acres.

I can save some of you a great deal of money and heartache if you ask me whether it's economical to move a house onto your property. It's not! But we did it. We dragged it onto our property, and it has taken us over five months to get it close to being legally habitable, according to city codes and standards. Hopefully by the time I get back home, my son and his family will be moving into it. But for now, they are living with us.

One of Tim's kids is five months old. So, we have a baby and an 82-year-old both under the same roof. When I walk through the dark living room at night, I don't know if I'm going to trip over a stroller or a wheelchair.

It has been a lot of fun.

We also have a little two-bedroom cottage on our property that we have used on and off for various forms of ministry. Most recently, we have let it stay empty in hopes of using it as a retreat for ministers. Then I came under conviction a couple of months ago. We shouldn't let it sit idle out there just so fat preachers can come to Florida for a free vacation. So, we found a homeless family. I mean, they were right off the streets, living under a tree. They're living in that little cottage now—the husband, wife, and three little children between the ages of 6 and 9.

One night, two weeks ago, one of those kids set our woods on fire. Applying a newfound book of matches to a fresh pile of pine needles was just too hard to resist. As we were stomping out the fire, I had to do a whole lot of soul-searching as to whether God had actually been the one convicting me or not.

When the fire department finally arrived, they squirted out the flames that by that time had gotten into the tops of the trees. It really wasn't as bad as it looked at night. Fires at night seem much worse than they really are.

I have learned a whole lot about this subculture of the homeless, since we now have these folks living with us. It's actually been a good experience for us. It really has. We're committed to helping this family reenter society after so many years of living on the streets in crack cocaine-infested communities.

For 12 years this couple has never filed an income tax return. The wife has never even gotten a social security number. She just makes one up as she goes from side-job to side-job. People ask her what her social number is, and she knows enough to rattle off nine random numbers.

The husband has spent most of his adult life running from society. He spent some time in prison, and when he got out, he found odd jobs but never bothered to pay any taxes. Now, after many years, he's afraid to file his return, because he's worried it will all catch up with him, and the IRS will come and put him in prison again. We've had to convince him that he needs to run that risk. In the process, we've discovered that he's actually got refund money coming back to him from the job he has now. It's a decent job and he's holding it down, making good progress.

It's been a good exercise, mostly, for us, and we have learned in the process. Even the fire in the woods was a good learning experience for everyone involved.

I used to be wary of homeless people. They were different. They were not like me. I would steer clear of them, thinking their "disease" might rub off on me. But as I have talked with this fellow and his family, I am beginning to see that they are not so unlike me after all. They just have a different background and different experiences.

EARLY FEARS

As far back as I can remember, I've also been afraid of Pentecostals. Pentecostals used to scare the *bejabbers* out of me. I can go all the way back to my childhood in the late 1930s and remember being frightened by a Pentecostal lady in my little hometown in Florida. My folks told me that people like her rolled on floors in their church and swung from light fixtures. I can hear my mother now: "Don't date a Catholic, and keep away from the Pentecostals."

So, I was very cautious about how I conducted myself as a child around people I thought were different. A couple of times I remember having nightmares about how the crazy Pentecostals might get me if I wasn't careful.

People inside the community church I attended as a kid were spiritually passive. But the Pentecostals down the street were very aggressive. When whatever they had somehow "got you," it would take you away and indoctrinate you into a strange culture.

Without warning you would start wearing checkered shirts, linen coats, striped pants, and white socks. You would become loud and boisterous, crude and ignorant. And you would always be out of control.

That was my initial image of Spirit-filled people—my childhood understanding of what it would be like to be filled with the Holy Ghost. Someday, if I didn't watch out, they would get me, and off I'd go.

Well, *they* didn't get me, but the Holy Spirit did. And I want to tell you how it happened.

I had known all along—even in my Southern Baptist days, when I was in seminary in the 1950s, and when I was pastoring Baptist churches in South Carolina and Florida in the 1960s—that there was more to this life-long walk with the Lord than I was experiencing. That I was just scratching at the edges of what God wanted for me. That there was a core of reality, of power and authority, that Jesus and His disciples had—and I didn't have it. In all my years as a dyed-in-the-wool Baptist, I knew there was more to the power of God than what I was experiencing. Not only did I not have it, but I didn't know anybody else who had it, either. Still, I knew deep down that whatever it was, it was available for everybody.

As I considered the life of Jesus and His disciples during my studies of the New Testament, I realized that none of the people who had Holy Spirit power were professional religionists. The preachers of the day didn't have it. And by preachers, I mean the professional religionists—the guys who got paid for being religious. The Pharisees didn't have it. The ones who had the real power of God were fishermen, tax collectors, common people, and one reformed whore.

These people had all come to Jesus, and somehow, they had received His power. They, in turn, took it out to other people—the folks who were sick and got healed, for example, or the folks who were filled with demons and were delivered. They were the evangelists of the day, not the guys who were dressed up all fancy and sleek, with massive meeting tents and gold-plated calling cards.

There was a subculture of that society that was somehow filled with God's power and God's authority. They had something—a power, a joy—that I didn't have. And I knew it.

But I didn't know why.

I didn't know what was wrong with me, so I bought into a specific theology, thanks to the Baptist seminary I attended.

Let me tell you this: one Southern Baptist seminary is like all the others. They all taught this doctrine at one time. I think most of them have backed off it now. But I was taught that the reason I didn't have what I knew was missing in my spiritual life was because the world was divided into "dispensations."

There was a dispensation—a period of time—when God visited people with power and authority and miracles. But that dispensation died out with the original apostles or at the end of the first century or some other undetermined time. In any case, it was over long before you and I came along. The power of the Holy Spirit that we read about in the New Testament doesn't exist anymore. That is what "dispensationalism" means. It means that now, today, we, the people of God, must depend upon our minds rather than upon the power of God—the power of the Holy Spirit.

Now we can figure things out. We are scientific. We are enlightened. We are advanced. We can handle things ourselves. We don't have to depend on miracles. We don't have to depend on God except in some odd, non-specific way—like the way the people of England depend upon the Queen. They parade her out every once in a while and say, "God save the Queen." But they really don't mean that. All they really want is for the Queen to stay out of the way, so they can do whatever they want to do.

Most churches are like that. They put up a big picture of Jesus in the back of the baptistry, or they hang a large wooden cross on the back wall, or something like that. But it doesn't mean anything to them. It's like a fig tree without figs—a lot of leaves and no fruit. That's how it was in my church. It always concerned me, even though I didn't know why.

Many times, when I stood up to preach in my Baptist church in South Carolina, I was afraid. I had this odd, ongoing fear that somebody—probably dressed in a robe, with twigs in his hair—would march in the front door, walk about halfway down the aisle, and shout "Fraud!"

I knew I had no answer to the accusation, because I knew that's what I was. I was speaking the words, but I was empty inside. I was like those huge stone lions I once saw at Trafalgar Square in London. They are set in the middle of a large fountain, with water coming out of their mouths. There's water enough for other people, but the lions themselves go thirsty, because they're made out of stone.

In the early days of my preaching, I felt as if I were made of stone. What I was saying was right and good, yet I knew there was more. There had to be more, because I was dying inside.

Following my traumatic experience at the writers' conference on Long Island, when my bush burned, I went home all the more certain that there was more to the Christian life than what I was experiencing.

My Long Island trip was in October of 1968. In November I was back in New York City, starting my research on the book that I had just signed a contract to write. It was going to be called *Run Baby Run*, and it was about Nicky Cruz, the New York City street gang member who had a miraculous encounter with Jesus. I didn't know it at that time, but that book was going to catapult both Nicky and me into a whole different kind of ministry, a dimension neither of us ever dreamed about.

Here I was—a bombed out, failed, besmirched Southern Baptist pastor walking the streets of New York with a Puerto Rican gang leader who could barely speak English. And we were going to write a book together. And the guy who arranged the deal was a Russian Pentecostal jeweler who lived in New Jersey.

So, I'm thinking, *What in the world is going on here? I didn't ask God for this.* I was afraid that if I did ask God what was happening, He might just tell me. Sometimes it's better to not ask questions. All I knew was that I was supposed to do whatever it was that came along. I had to. I really had no alternative.

HOW IT ALL BEGAN

We had started a tiny little church down in Florida. It was split out of the second church I'd been fired from. We started with about 60 people, including kids, but quickly dropped to 45, and we were moving rapidly in a downward direction. It was a dire situation. I knew I was going to have to do something other than pastor that tiny church to earn a living for myself, my wife, and our five kids.

The leaders of the church said they wanted to pay me $200 a week. But as a tiny congregation, we were only taking in $215 a week. With that, we couldn't even pay the rent or the light bill in our little building, a converted childcare facility. I knew we were in trouble. I knew I was going to have to do something, or my family and I would be out on the streets.

When the opportunity to write this book came along, I knew I had no choice but to sign the contract. And upon signing, the publisher gave me a $1,000 advance.

I had never gotten $1,000 for not doing anything yet.

Then the publisher paid my way back to New York to begin a series of interviews with Nicky Cruz. The first place we went was to the old, run-down Fort Greene section of Brooklyn, where the original Teen Challenge building had been located.

The idea was for Nicky to show me and our publisher, the Russian Pentecostal named Dan Malachuk, all his former haunts and hideouts from back in his gang-leader days in the late 1950s and early 1960s. So here I was, wearing a coat and tie and carrying a little notepad, trying to pretend I was a writer, following this former gang leader through the ghetto, and he was talking to all the guys and gals on the streets as if he were still one of them.

It was a wet, cold, rainy November afternoon. Some scary-looking young men were standing on a particular street corner, swinging chains, dressed in leather jackets with gang emblems on them. Nicky walked right up to these tough guys, pushed his way through them, and proceeded up a narrow stairway behind them. I'm thinking, *What in the world is a Southern boy like me doing here?*

All I really wanted to do was get out of that place. But I had signed a contract for a book deal. So up the stairs I went, with the guys with chains eyeing me all the way.

We were an odd trio: a tall Russian from New Jersey, a short little Puerto Rican who still carries a knife, and me.

We headed upstairs to the old Teen Challenge building. Nicky wanted to show me where he had gotten saved. The building was still being used as a drug addiction center, and addicts were coming and going everywhere.

It was cold and dreary, just above freezing, when we came back down the narrow set of steps. As we were about to head back into the rain, we saw a heroin addict who had dragged himself in off the street into the shelter of the stairwell. He was looking for help. A receptionist was normally at the front entrance, but he had left for a moment and was not there when this guy stumbled inside. He had only gotten as far as the bottom steps when he collapsed.

This fellow was a wretch of a man. He was lying across those steps, dry heaving, trying to vomit. But his stomach was empty. I couldn't tell how old he was. Heroin does that to people. He was soaked to the bone from the rain, and his shirt was sticking to his thin, emaciated back. He had no coat on, and the multiple sores all over the back of his neck and head were oozing pus. He was just lying there in this miserable situation, shaking, heaving, retching.

Dan was leading the way down the staircase, and he stepped over the guy. Nicky was next, but instead of stepping over him, he stopped for second. Since I was following Nicky, I had to stop, too. My initial thought was to get by the guy as quickly as possible. I didn't want to touch him or catch anything he had.

To my surprise, though, the Puerto Rican ex-gang leader stooped down beside the heroin addict and did something I'd never seen anybody do before. He reached over and laid his hand on that fellow. I mean, he didn't even hesitate to put his hand right on the back of his head, on top of those running sores with pus oozing everywhere.

Instantly the poor addict relaxed. He stopped heaving and gently fell asleep. And I heard a voice inside my head say, "That's what Jesus did for the lepers."

In all my sterilized preaching experiences, I'd never seen anybody touch anybody like that. I had heard about the "laying on of hands." We had done it in our church when we ordained deacons. All the new deacons would kneel at the altar, then the pastors would come along and lay hands on them—bald heads, burr haircuts, Vitalis, all nice and clean and well-groomed. That's what the laying on of hands was to me.

But I had never witnessed a true laying on of hands until I saw what this short, tough Puerto Rican did to this addict. Right in the middle of all that sin, he shared the power of God.

And then he began to pray in a language that I had never heard before. It wasn't Spanish. It wasn't English. It was just a prayer—in an unknown language.

I had never heard "tongues" before. My seminary professors used to talk about the heretics who spoke in tongues. We wouldn't even call it tongues. We would use the Greek term for it to dress it up: *glossolalia*. We used that term because most people can't pronounce it. We used it because we didn't want to face the fact that the Bible talks about "speaking in tongues" as something very real.

What Nicky did was not *glossolalia*. He spoke in tongues. He put his hands on that addict and prayed for him. It was a short prayer, in the Spirit, and then he moved on. He kept right on going, following Dan out the door.

And I was trapped. I couldn't move. In a split second, all the oxygen in the atmosphere had disappeared. It was like a vacuum. All the air was gone. But the power of God and the Spirit of God were there.

Later, I discovered the term *shekinah*. It's a word used when the High Priest would enter into the Holy of Holies on the Day of Atonement to pray for the nation of Israel. At that time the Holy Spirit would come, and the Jews referred to this visitation as the *shekinah*.

On those steps in that Brooklyn drug addiction center, I experienced the *shekinah*—the glory of God.

In all the prayer meetings I'd been in, all the preaching services I'd listened to, all the evangelistic meetings I'd sat through, all the great Baptist conferences I'd attended, I'd never experienced the *shekinah*. But I did that day in Brooklyn, when a Pentecostal Puerto Rican laid hands on a heroin addict's running sores and prayed in the Spirit.

Suddenly I knew I had found what I was looking for.

And I didn't want it.

I didn't want it, because I didn't want to lay hands on sick people. And I certainly didn't want to speak in tongues. I didn't want it, because I was afraid. I was afraid that if I did those things, I'd become like *them*.

Let me pause before I continue with this story. I want to tell you something, because it's extremely important that you catch this: God will never violate your personality. He will never make you be like anybody else. He doesn't want *you* to be like anybody else. God wants you to be like you are, like He created you to be. He wants you to be fulfilled. He wants you to become the very best of how He made you to be.

I didn't know that at the time. All I knew was how to act like other preachers. Now I thought I was going to become like somebody else again. I thought I was going to become like the Pentecostal appliance salesman I'd heard speak once, who put evangelistic tracts in the tubs of all his washing machines. I was afraid I was going to become like one of those guys—loud, rude, boisterous, arrogant, hopping up and down, and shouting at the top of my lungs.

I didn't want to be like that. And guess what? Neither did God.

God didn't want me to be like anybody else. He wanted me to be Jamie Buckingham, the way He meant for me to be from the Creation, from the foundations of the earth.

But, you see, I *wasn't* like Jamie. I was like everybody else. I was like my seminary professors. I was like my old pastor. I was even trying to be like Billy Graham. I was like all the people I admired. I wasn't like *me*, not the way God had created me. I was like everybody else, only I didn't know it.

God wanted to set me free from being like everybody else— and from being afraid of being like anybody else. He wanted to set me free from being intimidated by others. He wanted me to be the person He desired for me to be. But I didn't know that at the time. So, when Nicky finished praying, I stepped over the guy and got on out of there.

We found out the next day that the receptionist took the addict upstairs, where he slept all day and the next night. When he woke up, he was totally clean. No withdrawals. No cold-turkey shakes. Just clean.

I left the old Teen Challenge building and walked up to where Nicky and Dan were waiting in the cold, drizzling rain. They were laughing and talking about where to have lunch. And I said, "I don't understand how you fellas can be laughing out here. Didn't you see what took place back there?"

I thought we ought to be on our faces before God, stretched out prostrate like the old preachers sometimes did. I couldn't understand how they could be carrying on with life as usual, joking and kidding and talking about where to eat.

"How can you be acting like this?" I asked them.

Dan Malachuk turned and looked at me and said something extremely profound. He asked me a question. "Jamie," he said, "don't you Southern Baptists believe that God answers prayer?"

And suddenly I realized I did not. Not really. *Not really.* Oh sure, I prayed for people all the time. But I didn't have enough faith to believe that God would actually heal a heroin addict right there on those steps. I'd seen that guy with his emaciated body and running sores and listened to him as he heaved. I didn't think God would heal him. I thought he'd have to go to an institution, and the institution would heal him.

In our last session I mentioned that my father, after having been a churchman all his life, became a Christian when I was in college. My dad taught English literature at DePauw University in Greencastle, Indiana, before going into business in Florida. He was a reader, an intellectual. When he received the Lord, he got hold of J.B. Phillips' translation of the New Testament. He'd been trying to read the King James Version all his life and, like most everybody else, he couldn't understand it.

J.B. Phillips, the English scholar, had just finished a popular new translation titled *Letters to Young Churches*. My father marked it and marked it and marked it and marked it and marked it. Later, when I went into the ministry, he gave that Bible to me. In the front he had underlined the last sentence of the foreword that J.B. Phillips had written. After working through the Scriptures over and over again to get a more modern translation, Phillips came to this conclusion: "Perhaps if we believed what they believed, we might achieve what they achieved."

That's what was running through my mind in the backseat of the car as we drove through Brooklyn in that November rain. If I would believe what my Brooklyn companions believed—what the disciples in the early church believed—then what happened to them and through them would happen to me.

BABY STEPS IN THE SPIRIT

I went home from that interview searching. I asked everybody I could about the power of God. What could possibly account for the power I had witnessed that day in the stairwell?

Everybody I spoke to, outside of my normal circles, gave me the same answer. They said, "Why, it's the baptism in the Holy Spirit."

It was a term I'd never used before. I knew it was in the Bible, but I knew virtually nothing about it. It was what the Pentecostals in my hometown equated with the "second blessing," which my seminary professors said was heresy.

"There is no second blessing," they said, "not in this day and age." According to them, you got one blessing, and it just dribbled on for the rest of your life. And, of course, we all believed them.

But the folks I was now talking to were saying, "It's the baptism in the Holy Spirit. What you need, Jamie, is the baptism in the Holy Spirit. You mean you haven't been baptized in the Holy Spirit?"

They said it was the opening, the door, to becoming who God wants you to be. You can't really be who God wants you to be until you've been baptized in the Holy Spirit.

And I didn't know what that was.

Nor was I sure I wanted it. I still had images of folks who were dressed funny. The women had hair piled on top of their heads and didn't wear any lipstick or makeup. The men wore checkered shirts, and their pants were pulled up way too high. I got hung up on that image. These people didn't look right to me, so I didn't want to believe what they had to say.

But everyone kept giving me the same answer.

Two Pentecostal women came to my house one afternoon shortly after I got home from New York. They had heard there was a Baptist preacher in town who had been shot down, and he was starting a tiny little church called The Tabernacle. I guess they figured I was ripe for something new and fresh and different. They walked right up and knocked on the front door. I actually knew one of them. But they both scared me to death. Neither one of them had any makeup on. They both had their hair piled up in beehives on their heads. And they were stern-looking.

The day they came, my wife wasn't home. They marched right past me into the house and headed for my study. I had enclosed the garage and put in a desk and a small table so I could write in private, away from my five kids. Well, no sooner had they stepped foot in my makeshift study that they put their hands in the air and started walking around the room, praying in an unknown language.

All I could do was stand back and look at them. I couldn't believe what was happening. I had a picture of an airplane I used to own hanging on the wall. Quickly they became enchanted with that picture. When they walked by it, they'd go, "Ohhh, ahhh," and act all weird and funny.

And then they left.

My goodness, I thought. *Is that what becoming a Pentecostal does to you?* I didn't know.

The interesting thing was, I suddenly realized I no longer cared.

I was so hungry by that time for the power of God, for truth, for reality, that even if I became a freak, it was okay. I just knew there was more to this Spirit-led life, and somehow, I had to break through the barriers in my life and get on to where spiritual reality was.

The next February I went to Washington, D.C. I'd been up there once a couple of months earlier, when Nicky was speaking at a Full Gospel Businessman's Fellowship convention. This time he was speaking to the youth at another FGBMF convention. I needed one more interview to finish the book, so the plan was to meet up with him there. I had no idea what the Full Gospel Businessmen's Fellowship was. I thought they were like the Knights of Columbus for the Pentecostal church, except without the checkered coats and striped pants. I had no idea what to expect.

As it turned out, the convention was the wildest thing I had ever seen in all my life. It was at the Shoreham Hotel—a big, fancy, Washington hotel—and there were over 4,000 people attending from all across the Eastern seaboard. Everybody was carrying a Bible. They were shouting and praising the Lord up and down the sidewalks outside. They were witnessing to the cab drivers and to the junkies out on the street, and even to a couple of foreign ambassadors who happened to be staying at the hotel. I couldn't even register at the desk, because they were handing out tracts to the girl who was trying to get everyone registered. I mean, it was wild and crazy.

The hotel lobby was packed with people, all saying "Hallelujah!" and "Praise the Lord!" I had never heard those terms used outside of a church building. We never used those terms, except when we sang specific songs or played Handel's "Messiah" on the record player. It was okay to say "hallelujah" then, but only in those limited circumstances. Yet here they were, using it like it was common vocabulary.

And hugging people? I'd never been hugged by a man before. Even my own daddy rarely hugged me.

I didn't know what to make of it all. It was like walking into an entirely different culture and speaking a different language. People were acting different. It was crazy. And yet, somehow, I knew there was a bottom line of reality to this. These people were free. They were uninhibited. They were themselves. I wasn't sure I liked it, but they were definitely being themselves! They had reached that place of becoming who God had intended for them to be. They weren't bound up by convention or by conventional ways of doing things. They were free.

The first afternoon I was there, I found myself in a big Bible study. David du Plessis was speaking to this huge crowd of a few thousand people. David was an old-time Pentecostal who was consorting with popes and cardinals. God was using him to build bridges between Catholics and Pentecostals and Protestants. I was sitting in the front row, and I couldn't understand a word he was saying. He was speaking English, of course, teaching from Ephesians. People all around me had their notebooks and Bibles out. They were saying "hallelujah" and praising the Lord and making notes. And there I was, with my seminary education, and I couldn't understand him. Nothing he said was making any sense to me.

It was a little later that I began to realize that, until the Holy Spirit is inside of you, the Bible really doesn't make much sense. It's just another book with a lot of long words in it. But once you've had an experience with the One who wrote that book, then you begin to understand everything it says.

And I had not had that experience yet. Oh sure, I was a follower of Jesus, but I was not filled with the same Spirit that filled Jesus. I was not leading a Spirit-led life. But I was searching, and I was longing for it.

So, I just sat there. And just about the time David was getting ready to finish, the master of ceremonies stood up. He was actually the brother of my Russian Pentecostal friend, and he was crazier than his brother. His name was Earl Malachuk.

Earl came down off the platform to where I was sitting and said to me, "Brother, God just spoke to me."

And I said to him, "What do you mean God just spoke to you? What did He say?"

"God said that you're to sing a solo as soon as David du Plessis finishes preaching."

"You have got to be kidding," I said. "I sing in the shower. Sometimes I lead praise and worship in my church. But in front of 2,000 people I don't know? You want me to come up there and . . ."

"That's right," Earl said. "God has spoken. Hurry up and get ready, because as soon as David finishes, I'm calling you up to the platform." Then he walked back to his seat on the platform, sat down, and grinned at me.

I realized he meant business. David was winding down. Next it was going to be my turn.

I didn't know what to do. What do you do in a situation like that? I noticed there was an organ over to the side, and a guy was sitting on the bench. I got up from my seat and walked to the back of the auditorium, around the last row of seats, and down the other side to the man at the organ. I whispered to him, saying, "They just told me I'm supposed to sing."

"Hallelujah, brother!" he smiled.

I said, "I don't have any music."

"Well, praise God, neither do I."

"Don't you use music?"

"No. God gives me the notes, and I just play."

"Jeez!" I said. "What am I going to sing? I can't think of the words to anything."

I was stumped. I couldn't even think of the words to "Jesus Loves Me." My mind was totally blank. And now David had finished speaking and was sitting down.

The organist spoke to me again. "Can you remember the words to *How Great Thou Art?*"

"If you'll play it while I'm walking up there, maybe that will help me remember."

So he began to play by ear as I walked up to the microphone, and—*oh, dear Jesus!*—I just stood there and closed my eyes and started to sing.

I could remember the first stanza. But as I sang it, I knew I was going to be lost as soon as it was over, because for the life of me I couldn't remember the rest of the song.

"Oh Lord, my God . . . Oh Lord, my God . . ." And I'm thinking ahead. *What am I going to do when I finish this short first stanza? I'll sing the chorus, but I don't know anything that follows.*

I knew I couldn't remember, but I just went ahead anyway. When I was about to finish, I suddenly realized something bizarre had happened. I had had my eyes closed. I didn't want to see what was going on out there in the audience. But as the organ began to play the second verse, I opened my eyes, and all those people had their hands up and their eyes closed, tears on their faces, and they were singing. They had actually taken the song away from me. They went ahead and sang the next verse and the chorus and the next verse after that.

Then everything shifted, and they all began to sing a different song, one I'd never heard before. They were singing it in a language I didn't understand.

So, I got off the platform and went back to where I had been sitting.

The entire week was made up of that kind of unexplainable stuff. I was off in a whole new world—a world of being led by the Spirit. And I didn't know how to handle it.

The last afternoon of the conference, I decided to attend another one of the huge Bible studies. I knew I needed to get some answers before the convention was over. Again, about 2,000 people were there.

Off to the side I saw a group of the conference leaders heading up to the platform. I said to myself, *I've got to talk to somebody about what is happening here. But I'm afraid to talk to one of these Pentecostal types.*

I noticed that some of the wives of these men had spotted me already. I could see them coming across the hotel lobby. I knew what they wanted. They wanted to get hold of my tongue. If they could get hold of my tongue, if they could pull it out far enough, it would pop back like a window shade, and behold! I would speak in other languages.

No. I had to talk to somebody that I felt wasn't going to sit on me—somebody I wasn't afraid of.

I spotted an Episcopal priest sitting up on the platform. He was wearing his turned-around clerical collar. He was quiet and mild-mannered. *That guy looks like he's half-sane*, I thought. So, after the Bible study, I approached him. I didn't know what to call him. I was taught to never call a man "Father" because the Bible says, "Don't call any man father." As far as I knew, that meant to not even call your own father "father." I didn't know what to do. So, I said, "Excuse me. I need to talk to you about the Holy Spirit."

He replied, "What do you mean?"

"Well, people tell me I need to be baptized in the Spirit, and I want to know what they are talking about."

"Let's have dinner together," he said kindly.

"Fine. We'll have dinner."

"Meet me in the dining room, here at the hotel, tonight at 6."

TRAPPED BY THE SCRIPTURES

That evening I met him in the dining room. We sat down at the table, with nice silverware and china and crystal and a waiter hovering over us to take our order.

The Episcopal priest looked at me and said, "What do you want to know about the Holy Spirit?"

I said, "I'm a Southern Baptist pastor, and all of this is foreign to me."

He said, "You're a Southern Baptist?"

"Yes."

"Hallelujah!" Then he reached underneath the table and pulled out a huge Bible about eight times bigger than mine. He cleared away the silver and the china and the crystal, put that Bible down, and said, "I've been waiting to get hold of a Baptist for a long time."

I looked at the poor waiter who was standing there and watched him drift away from the table, while this priest started flipping pages and talking about the Scriptures.

He said, "The reason I've wanted to talk to a Baptist is because you are some of the only ones who really believe the Bible. I get hold of all these Episcopalians and Catholics and Methodists and Presbyterians. I never do know where they stand. But you Baptists, you believe the Bible. I want to show you some things that are written in this Bible."

"Well, go to it," I said.

"Let's look at Mark 16."

I said, "Okay. That's a good passage. I preach mission sermons from Mark 16. 'Go ye into all the world and preach the good news to all creation.'"

He said, "Have you ever read on beyond that part?"

"No, you don't need to read on beyond that," I told him. "That's a good mission text right there. That's as far as I've ever needed to go."

"'And these signs will accompany those who believe,'" he said as he read the verse that followed. He looked at me and said, "Do you believe?"

"Yes," I replied. "I believe."

"'In my name, they will drive out demons . . .'" he continued reading.

It was then I knew I was in trouble. I didn't believe in demons.

"'. . . and they will speak in new tongues.'"

I stopped him before he got to the part about snakes. I said, "Listen, one of the advantages of having a seminary education is you begin to learn which passages of Scripture are spurious and which are not. I've got a little footnote in my Bible that says, 'The most reliable early manuscripts don't have Mark 16:9-20 in them.' You're not going to hang me on a passage of Scripture that might not have been in the early manuscripts."

He said, "No problem. What about John 14? Do you believe John 14 is spurious?"

"No, no, no, no," I said. "That's where I get my funeral sermon from. John 14 is good."

"Fine. Let's go to John 14. 'I tell you the truth. Anyone who has faith in Me'... Do you have faith in Jesus?"

"I have faith in Jesus."

"'Anyone who has faith in Me will do what I have been doing. He will do even greater things than Me because I'm going to My Father,'" he read. Then he asked, "Are you doing greater things than Jesus?"

In that moment I realized I was a lot better off in Mark 16 than I was in John 14.

I was trapped by the Scriptures.

This book was the foundation of my life. I had based everything in my life on this book, even though I had not been able to live up to it. And now I was trapped by the book itself. I was trapped by the words of Jesus and the power of the Word of God.

I don't think we ever got dinner that night. I can't remember eating anything. I don't think the waiter ever came back. But we wound up in the ninth chapter of the Book of Acts. And I was arguing. I was throwing all my arguments at this Episcopal priest—the same arguments my Baptist professors had used on us inquisitive students back in seminary.

It's interesting when you're searching for something and you're afraid, because you're right at the door of where it may be. You begin to throw up defenses and dig in your heels. It's just about there, and you're afraid to move into it.

I threw up every defense I could—every theological defense and argument I could come up with: There is no second blessing. There is nothing beyond the initial rebirth experience. All you do is accept Jesus, and from that time on you grow in grace.

Then, as the Episcopal priest led me through the Scriptures that night at that dinner table, we got to Acts 9. It's the story of Paul's conversion on the road to Damascus.

"Do you believe that Paul had an experience with Jesus Christ on the road to Damascus?" he asked me.

"Oh, yes," I said. "I really do believe that with all my heart."

"Then let's take a look at this."

Together we read the story about how Paul got knocked off his horse and how, three days later, in the city of Damascus, the Holy Spirit spoke to a man across town by the name of Ananias.

> The Lord told him, "Go to the house of Judas on Straight Street and ask for a man from Tarsus named Saul, for he is praying. In a vision he has seen a man named Ananias come and place his hands on him to restore his sight." (Acts 9:11-12)

This was three days after Paul's conversion. Ananias argued with God, just like I was arguing with God. Then Ananias gave in and did what God asked him to do.

> Then Ananias went to the house and entered into it. Placing his hands on Saul, he said, "Brother Saul, the Lord—Jesus, who appeared to you on the road as you were coming here— has sent me so that you may see again and be filled with the Holy Spirit." (Acts 9:17)

It was a separate Holy Spirit experience. I had never seen it before. There it was. And once again, I was trapped by the Book.

I would not have responded to all the emotionalism of the Pentecostals. I would not have responded to everything they said and did. The only thing I was going to respond to was the Word of God.

And my heart opened. That very wise priest had enough sense to leave it right there. He didn't try to sell me. He didn't close the net. He didn't ask me to sign a card. He didn't say, "Can I pray for you?" He just left me alone. He had enough sense to know that God would do the work sovereignly once the right words had been planted.

MEETING THE HOLY SPIRIT

We broke off the conversation and parted company. It was time to go to the big meeting that night—the convention's closing session. I'm not going to go into all the details of what happened that evening or the miracles that took place. But I'll tell you this. They changed the speaker at the very last minute. They had a Pentecostal preacher set up to preach, but they canceled him, because a Southern Baptist pastor by the name of Johnny Osteen had flown up from Houston.

Johnny said, "God spoke to me in Houston and told me to get on a plane and fly to Washington, D.C. He told me I was to be the closing-night speaker at the Full Gospel Businessmen's Convention."

He wasn't even on the program. Yet, when he showed up, completely unannounced, the leaders prayed and agreed. "Yes, God has spoken."

They canceled the man who was scheduled to speak and allowed Johnny Osteen to close out the convention. And because he was a Southern Baptist, he was the only man I would have heard.

I have thought back to that situation time and time again, and I am prepared to say I believe God arranged the entire convention for me alone. Sure, there were 4,000 people there. But I believe it was arranged simply for me. Nobody else. Others may have been blessed, they may have gotten some spillover, but it was *my* convention, because it was my time to understand what it meant to be filled and led by the Spirit.

I came in that night, and the only place to sit was on the third row. The entire ballroom was packed. Everyone was there to hear Johnny Osteen. He picked his Bible up, opened it, and began to speak.

And I responded to the Word of God.

A man two seats down from me stood up in the middle of the message. He interrupted the message with a prophecy. I didn't know anybody ever did that kind of thing. But the room was so packed with the power of the Holy Spirit that it didn't make any difference. He just picked up where Johnny Osteen was preaching and prophesied for a minute, then sat back down. Johnny continued on without a hitch.

The prophecy was only a parenthetical in the midst of a sermon—but it was directed towards me. I later got a copy of the prophecy, because I got a copy of the transcript of the whole service. The message was directed to my heart. It was God saying, "I have a man here tonight that I have chosen."

I couldn't hear the rest of the sermon, because I was so overcome by what I had heard in that short prophetic word. At the close of the service, Johnny gave an invitation. It was a scriptural invitation: "Everyone who wants to receive Jesus, come on down."

And they came. A lot of them.

Then he gave a second invitation. He said, "There's another experience called the baptism in the Holy Spirit. Those who want to be baptized in the Holy Spirit, come on down."

I gave my last little gasp of resistance and said to myself, *I've got to get out of here.*

People were moving all over the place. I squeezed out of my row of chairs and got over to an aisle just as Johnny said, "Now, I want the rest of you folks to form a wall of prayer around these people who are down here. Everybody come on down, and let's pray for these folks."

I looked up and saw 4,000 people coming down the aisle towards me. I couldn't make it out, so I just found a chair and sat down.

It was utter bedlam. All over the place, people were praying. Folks were on their knees, crying. Everybody was getting right with God somehow. And I was in the middle of it all.

I couldn't go down front. I couldn't be part of all those folks at the altar who were whooping and hollering and praying and crying. I couldn't do that. I didn't cry. I had my emotions completely under control. I didn't even cry at my older brother's funeral. He had died just a year before, and he didn't know the Lord. I couldn't weep or grieve. I was under control. I was a controlled individual.

But that was part of the bondage, too. I was controlled by what others thought about me. I was like everybody else.

I thought, *What am I going to do? I have to sit here, because I can't get out. So, I might as well pray.*

I can remember sitting in that chair and putting my head in my hands. And suddenly it was that same experience I'd had on the steps in Brooklyn. *Shekinah.*

I couldn't believe it. It was like the time I had thrown a bucket of gasoline on a little fire. I didn't know it was gasoline. The explosion had sucked all the oxygen out of the air, and I couldn't catch my breath. Now I was sitting there, and all the air was gone again.

Yet, He was there, in all His power and all His glory, and I was closeted in with Him.

I began to cry. I wept. And wept. I convulsed in tears, and I didn't care who saw me or heard me. It didn't make any difference. It was just me and God.

Then I felt a hand touch my shoulder. It was the Episcopal priest, who had somehow found me in the middle of all the confusion. He just put his arm on my shoulder and said, "Jamie, is it real?"

I tried to describe to him what was happening. The only description I could come up with was, it's like when you take the cover off one of those old-time golf balls. They're wound tight inside with tiny bands of rubber. And when you put a razor blade to them, they start peeling away. Everything starts to fall way. That's what was happening to my life right then.

The kindly priest said, "Those are the chains that are coming off. You are being set free."

I don't know how long I was sitting there crying. The priest left me after a while, and somehow I made my way up to my room. I called my wife. That seemed to be the right thing to do. Our marriage relationship had been really strained following that affair . . . *affairs.* Jackie had committed herself to stay with me, but we were just barely walking together.

I felt God say, "Call her." So I called her and woke her up. It was midnight, and I was crying over the phone. I said, "I love you." I had not told her that—except to lie to her—in a long time. And she knew something had happened.

She was the only person who really counted to me at that moment. I didn't care about what anybody else thought. But she knew.

BRINGING THE SPIRIT HOME

The next morning, I got on a plane and flew home. Always before I had kept my Bible in my briefcase. But that morning I put it in my lap. I wanted somebody to notice it. I wanted somebody to ask me about that book.

I found myself witnessing to a girl who said she was a student at the University of Maryland at College Park. I had never witnessed to anybody, except when I went out to knock on neighborhood doors on Tuesday nights with membership cards in hand. But this was so real, so spontaneous.

I got home Saturday night and stayed up all night long confessing to my wife. I couldn't keep it in any longer—the lies, the hypocrisy. And Jackie and I worked through it all that night.

The next morning was Sunday. I went in front of my tiny little church of 40 or 50 people and told them what took place in Washington, D.C. I said to them, "I don't know what has happened to me, but it's God." And I began to cry again.

In fact, for the next two years, every time I talked about Jesus, I cried. I couldn't stand in the pulpit and mention His name without crying.

That morning I told the people, "I don't know what has happened. I don't know what God is doing or where He's taking us. All I can say is, I think He wants this for you, too."

When I finished, I sat down. Then everybody in that little church—all of them with Southern Baptist roots—got up out of their chairs, came forward, and knelt on the floor in the tiny little building where we were meeting.

And they began to cry, too.

They said, "Whatever it is you have, we want it, too. Because it's real. We are tired of the phony. We want what is real."

I didn't know what to do with them. I just had to let them kneel there and cry. And I went on home.

Back at the house, my wife said she wanted me to pray for her. She said, "Lay hands on me so I can have it, too."

I didn't know how to do that. I didn't know how to lay on hands for *this*. So, I told her, "Whatever God did to me, He will have to do it to you, too."

Three weeks later she woke me up in the middle of the night, shouting and yelling. God had visited her in a dream and baptized her in the Holy Spirit. She was up all the rest of the night, walking through the house, shouting and yelling, "Hallelujah!"

We've been shouting and yelling "hallelujah!" ever since.

I didn't speak in tongues then. It was three years later before I spoke in tongues. That really bothered my Pentecostal friends. They didn't think I'd really had an experience with the Holy Spirit, because I didn't immediately speak in tongues. But it didn't make any difference to me. I was so filled with the Spirit that I didn't have room for anything else. It wasn't until much later that I began to say, "Lord, I want everything, including *that*." It's a whole other story I'll get to later.

I realize now it is part of the package. I believe now, looking back, that I could have spoken in tongues that last night of the convention in the Shoreham Hotel. I just didn't need to. In fact, I really believe God withheld it from me on purpose, because since then, nearly everybody I have laid hands on to receive the baptism in the Holy Spirit has spoken in tongues. We came to the place after a while that I was the only person in our church who didn't speak in tongues.

But that was God's method, because that kept me safe. If I'd come back from the convention blubbering in tongues, everybody who was left in the church would have run away.

But God was gentle with them. He allowed them to receive only what they could receive, in their time—in His time. And finally, in my time, too.

CRITICAL TIMES FOR THE CHURCH

I believe God is moving. He's cranking up the timetable. I believe He is saying to us now, "These are the most critical days in the history of the church."

These days are more critical than the days of the first century church. We are under the same kind of political pressure, religious pressure, demonic pressure, that the first century church was under, only now we're a million times bigger. Only now we're in every nation of the world. Only now the kingdom is spread throughout every tribe in every language. Only now God's people are everyplace, and the pressure that is coming upon the kingdom is greater than it has ever been. It has become mandatory, as far as I am concerned, to be filled with the Holy Spirit in order to be effective.

In my understanding of the Scripture, it is absolutely mandatory that we be filled with the same Spirit that Jesus was filled with. We cannot continue with our church games. We can't continue playing our roles. God wants us to become who we really are. He has created us for a purpose. He has placed dreams and visions within our hearts.

He has gifts He wants to give to us. He wants to fill us with His Holy Spirit, so that all He desires for us is activated inside of us. It is there. And He wants to activate it now. He has breathed into us His image, and now He is breathing into us His life.

We are like the valley of dry bones that God brought to life. God has breathed upon a mighty army that is standing up and marching forward. God is saying, "I have something for you. And I have something not only for you individually; I have something for you corporately that you will experience in the realm of the church, in the fellowship of the community—something that you could never experience individually.

"It is for you. And as you go together, as you march together, I will do something powerful in you and for you, and I will go before you. And you will see My hand in ways that you never imagined. But you must be equipped. You must be empowered. You must be filled with My Spirit."

Everything I have said up to this point is to get to the place of saying this: God wants to do it *now*. He wants to fill you with His Spirit *now*.

Suddenly it becomes very personal, doesn't it? Suddenly your mouth has gone dry. I know what you must be thinking: *Up until this time, he was talking about himself. Now he is talking about me.*

That's right.

But God is gentle, and He will not force you. He will allow it to happen to you as you have desire for it, as you are ready for it. The Holy Spirit is a gentleman. He will knock on your door, but He will not bash it down. And even if you open it, He will not drag you out into His territory. He will wait until you invite Him into yours.

But once you invite Him in, He will come in with everything He has.

I was so afraid that if I allowed the Holy Spirit to take control of my life, I would speak in tongues, I would preach from street corners, I would prophesy before strangers, I would dance up and down the aisles. I would do all the things that the back-country Pentecostals did in my little Florida town back in the 1930s.

I want to tell you something. Everything that I feared—*everything*—has come upon me.

But let me assure you of this: *nothing* has happened in my life of being led by the Spirit that He has not first given me the desire for.

Whatever happened to me, I wanted it first. Over time, it became my desire. God did not force Himself in any way on me. But the vacuum inside of me had become so great that I wanted Him to fill it more than anything. And when He came in, He came in with all His holiness and all His power and all His authority.

He has given me a fearlessness that I never dreamed could be mine.

WANTING GOD

I'm going to assume something right now. I'm going to assume that you want all God has for you. I'm going to assume that you wouldn't have come this far with me if you didn't want access to the full power of the Holy Spirit. Otherwise, you would be off to some other church, playing little church games. And believe me, there are a lot of games being played in churches today.

Perhaps you've already been tagged as something of an oddity by your friends or family. Perhaps that's why you're here. Because this *is* different. This is not like everybody else.

So, based on this assumption that you really want all that God has for you, I'll tell you what's next: you need to be filled with the Holy Spirit.

Remember, Jesus breathed upon His disciples before He left them. He said, "My Spirit is the only thing I'm going to leave behind. I'm not going to leave a church behind. I'm not going to leave an institution behind. I'm not going leave a training program behind. I'm not going to leave anything behind but My Spirit. That's all. But if you have that, if you have My Spirit, then that's all you will ever need."

The Holy Spirit will interpret the Word for you. He will give you the power for miracles. He will give you wisdom and discernment for walking through this world. He will give you good sense for handling business deals. He will provide for you. He will make a way through the wilderness for you. He will become the all-in-all in your life, your business, and your home.

I encourage you to take the opportunity to accept Him now. Ask the Holy Spirit to come into your life. You don't need an altar call. You don't need anyone else to pray with you. All you need is to have an open heart and a willingness to let the Spirit of God move into your life.

It may not hit you until sometime later. It may not really impact you until you turn the lights out and have your head on your pillow tonight. But just as you are drifting off to sleep, He will be there in a deep new way, because you have invited Him in.

Let me assure you of another thing: if you invite Him in, He *will* come in. If you invite Him in with an open and sincere heart, He will come in. If you ask, if you seek, if you knock—your Heavenly Father will not give you a snake if you ask for a fish. He will not give you a stone if you ask for bread. He will give you the

Holy Spirit if you ask Him for the Holy Spirit. Even if you don't verbally ask for Him, He will read your heart.

Sitting up there in Washington, D.C., that late Friday night, I didn't ask for anything. But God read my heart. I couldn't voice it with my lips. I still didn't know what to ask for or what to say. But He read my heart, and that was enough. He did it because He is God. And He will do it that way for you, too, right where you are.

Receiving the Holy Spirit is making Jesus the Lord of your life. I don't want to get tangled up with all the definitions of what that means. I don't understand them. I really don't. And I don't trust people who say they do. There are a whole lot of things having to do with God that are mysteries—great mysteries.

All I'm asking you to do is to say, "Lord, I want everything You have for me." Then I want you to take an additional step. I want you to step out in faith and be willing to allow all the things that happened to the early believers happen to you, as well.

At Pentecost, when all the believers came together at that first Pentecostal meeting in the upper room, the Spirit came upon them—all of them, even Jesus' mother, Mary—and they all spoke in tongues as the Spirit gave them utterance. Notice, *they* spoke, and the Spirit gave them utterance. You still have to cooperate with God.

I don't believe that tongues is the initial evidence of the Holy Spirit coming into a person's life. I don't know what the initial evidence is.

Jesus did say, "You will be witnesses unto Me." That's an initial evidence.

For me, it was joy and freedom. That was the initial evidence for me. Telling my wife I loved her was my initial evidence. That was more important to God than anything else. Speaking in tongues came down the road.

I don't know what the initial evidence will be for you. But whatever it is, God wants to give it to you. He will give His gifts to you as He wills. And there *will* be an evidence that follows. It will be there. You will know, and you will receive it by faith— simply because you asked for it.

And your life, from that point forward, will never be the same.

CHAPTER 3

TAKING DOMINION

I want to tell you two stories that took place on different sides of the world.

Several years ago, I was invited by a Filipino pastor, Aley Gonzales, to come minister to his little congregation on the island of Mindanao, which is the southernmost big island of the Philippine archipelago. I agreed, not knowing exactly what to expect.

Aley was very poor. He had a motorbike that he rode all over the northern part of the island, preaching the gospel. I spent ten days with him in his house built on stilts, with a thatched roof and mosquito nets for windows. His was a very simple, Bible-oriented ministry. We talked about the power of the Holy Spirit. We talked about miracles and faith. It was a good time.

The following year, I went back to Mindanao, this time taking a friend with me. It was good to spend more time with Aley.

While we were there the second time, Aley told me a remarkable story. In fact, he had his eight-year-old son, Fernando, tell me the story.

Fernando attended a very poor public school. It was a one room schoolhouse with a concrete floor and no screens in the windows. There were no desks—just chairs with little boxes in front of them—and only one teacher for everyone. The school was so poor, the students had to bring their own pencils and paper.

One day it came time for an examination. Fernando had studied very hard for the test, but he didn't have a pencil. He had a sheet of paper but no pencil. So, the teacher wouldn't let him take the exam. Instead, she made him go sit outside.

Fernando was heartbroken. He had studied hard, and he knew all the answers. He sat down on the stump of a palm tree, and he began to cry.

As he cried, he took his piece of paper and rolled it up, like a little kid would do. Then he unrolled it. He sat there on that stump with the paper, rolling it up, unrolling it, rolling, unrolling, over and over.

It was then that he remembered what I had said in my sermon earlier in the week—about who God is and how He supplies your needs, and that miracles are possible.

He began to pray a simple prayer: "Lord, I need a pencil." Suddenly he felt something hard inside the rolled sheet of paper. He unrolled it, and there was a big yellow pencil with an eraser on one end and a sharpened point on the other end.

He was so excited! He went back into the classroom and told the teacher he had a pencil now. She let him take the exam, which he passed.

After Fernando told us his story, he went back to his little corner of the house, grabbed the very same pencil, and showed it to me. It was just an ordinary wooden pencil, with an eraser and a metal band and no writing on it.

He called it his "miracle pencil." I wonder why?

The second story comes from the other side of the world. It happened seven years ago, when I was in the Sinai Desert. I had taken a group of men with me as I was doing research on a book I was writing, *A Way Through the Wilderness*. I had been to the Sinai a number of times before, doing research, following the footsteps of Moses. You may have seen the Bible video series we taped while on some of those trips to Israel.

On this particular trip, I had a group of 10 men with me, and we were making our way across the Sinai Peninsula. Most of the men had never met each other before coming on this journey with me. We had a desert vehicle, and were heading to a place called Serabit el-Khadim, which is on the eastern side of the Sinai. It's where there once were huge turquoise mines. There had been a landslide recently across the dirt road we were traveling on, so we had to make a detour.

There we were, driving this old six-wheel desert vehicle, and we're all bouncing around in the back, enjoying the beautiful serenity of the desert landscape with our Israeli guide and Israeli driver.

On the little detour, we came upon a Bedouin camp. The Bedouins are nomadic people who live in tents and herd sheep and goats. There were only three tents in the camp, with some children running around. As we were about to pass by, a man came running toward us. As it turned out, I had met this man before on one of my earlier journeys through the desert. His name was Bakarat. He had been appointed by the Egyptian government as the caretaker over that whole area of Serabit el-Khadim.

Bakarat came running out with his robe and turban on, waving his arms. So, we stopped and got out. There had been an accident in the camp the week before. Bakarat's little boy, who was maybe a year old, had reached up and pulled down a teapot full of boiling water. The water had poured over his head and horribly burned the whole front part of his head and face. Over the past week that scalded skin had partially scabbed over and become terribly infected. His wound covered everything from the top of the middle part of his head all the way down to his eyebrows and all the way back to his ears. It was oozing with pus and the flies were everyplace, in the child's nose and eyes and on the scab.

The father and mother were deeply concerned, of course, because the child was now feverish. They wanted to know if we had a doctor in our little group. Well, it so happened that we did have a medical doctor with us. He had come along as we were camping, cooking our own food, and sleeping in sleeping bags out underneath the stars.

So, I asked my doctor friend if he would mind looking at this terribly wounded little boy. He agreed. After a few minutes, he came out of the tent and shook his head. "I don't know what I can do," he said. "I've got some medicine, some salve, but it won't do any good. The child needs to be hospitalized. He needs to have that scab softened and removed, in order to treat the infection underneath. I just don't know what I can do without proper equipment and antibiotics."

Also in our group was a big, tall Messianic Jew named Mike

Evans. Mike is something of a wild man from Fort Worth, Texas. He's got an opinion on just about everything. He's outspoken and brash, and we remain good friends to this day.

Mike stepped forward as he watched what was happening. "All we have to do is pray for this child," Mike said.

"Mike, these are Muslims," I replied, "and the father is standing over there, and he's got a knife in his belt that's huge." And it was. It had a curved point on the end and a jewel in the middle of the handle.

But Mike persisted. "Let's just pray in the name of Jesus."

"Mike," I objected, "our Jewish guides are watching. And the Muslim people in this little tent village are gathering."

But Mike pushed his way through to the child. I couldn't stop him. Finally, I turned to the Jewish guide and said, "We are going to pray. Can you interpret in Arabic to this father, so he knows what we're doing?"

Our guide, whom I'd known from past trips, said, "You want to pray in the name of Jesus, don't you?"

"Yes," I said. "We're going to pray in the name of Jesus."

Our guide knew me, and he guessed correctly. But still he got a little nervous. "Aren't there enough problems between Jews and Arabs as it is, without injecting Jesus into the whole picture?" he said with a wry smile.

He finally relented and told the father, Bakarat, what we were going to do. To our surprise, the father was desperate enough to get help for his son that he agreed. He gave us the okay to pray in the name of Jesus.

"Go ahead," he said through our Jewish guide who was interpreting for us. "If you can't do anything else, at least do that."

So, we all gathered inside the tent and laid hands on this sick, feverish child while his father held him. We laid hands on the boy and prayed in the name of Jesus: "Lord, heal this child. Please."

And that was it.

We got back in our vehicle and took off. We went on and found the mountains we wanted to climb and spent a couple of days there. Later we returned the same way we came. It was our intention to head further south into the high granite mountains where Mount Sinai is.

As we passed through Bakarat's Bedouin camp, he came out again, waving his arms. We stopped the vehicle, and I said to the guys, "If that child has died, we'd better start saying our own prayers, because we're in trouble."

But no—Bakarat was all smiles. "Come, come, come," he beckoned, gesturing for us to follow him. So, we got out of the vehicle and went into his little tent. There, in his mother's arms, was the child. The horrible scab was gone, and in its place was new pink flesh. The doctor inspected him and found no signs of infection. None.

All we had done was pray—and leave the rest in God's hands.

WHAT GOD REALLY SAID

Two stories: one in the Philippines, one in the Sinai Peninsula. For years, I had read stories like that. I had read books written by other people telling stories like that. In fact, I read the Bible. It's got a lot of stories like that in it. But I didn't believe them. And the reason I didn't believe them was because I had never seen any miracles for myself.

I read all the stories of Jesus' miracles. I read them in seminary as an adult, and I read them in Sunday school as a boy. But I looked upon those stories the same way I looked upon other made-up stories—like the kid whose mother sent him into town to sell the family cow, but he traded it for some lousy beans instead.

Remember that story? When Jack came home, his mother got upset and threw the beans out the window. The next morning, they saw that from those beans, a huge stalk had grown all the way up into the clouds. So, Jack climbed the stalk and discovered that an evil giant lived up there, along with a goose that laid golden eggs.

I looked upon the stories in the Bible the same way I looked upon "Jack and the Beanstalk." They seemed like fairy tales from a time long past. They were not for today. Sure, they were nice, and they made you feel good. I was glad to have read them. But somehow the stories didn't apply to me. I had never seen a miracle.

When I went off to seminary in Ft. Worth, my professors—bless their hearts—went to great lengths to explain why those miracles happened in the New Testament. They happened to draw crowds, one professor claimed. They didn't have public address systems back then. They didn't have newspapers or television. So, God allowed a few miracles to take place, so people would come and listen to Jesus as He preached.

Peter and John went into the temple and laid their hands on a man who was lame. He jumped up, leaping and walking, and went through the temple proclaiming his healing. That was just an advertisement for the preaching service Peter and John were holding later, my professor said.

Miracles are not necessary anymore. Now we can take out ads in the newspaper. We can rent blimps to fly over the towns with flashing lights. We can do all sorts of other things to bring attention to our services and our sermons. We really don't need miracles in this day and age.

Yet, I was concerned. I was concerned, because I belonged to a church that proclaimed, "We are people of the Book. Where the Bible speaks, we speak."

There was a little slogan we used in our Baptist churches: "God said it. I believe it. That settles it."

But what did God really say? I didn't know what to do with so many of the things I read in the Bible. I didn't know how to clip out the miracles and then come up with a rationale to explain why they weren't valid for today. Didn't we claim to believe every word of the Scriptures?

I also struggled with other passages, like what the book of Hebrews says about Jesus being the same "yesterday, today and forever." If He's the same yesterday, today and forever, and if He is indeed alive today as we believe, and if He is in fact resurrected, then why had miracles stopped?

Finally, I reached a conclusion—despite what the denominational churches were teaching. Miracles hadn't stopped. I just hadn't seen them.

THE STORM OF ALL STORMS

I want to tell you a story from Mark chapter 4. It's a very familiar story about how Jesus calmed the storm while crossing the Sea of Galilee. It's a story about a power encounter.

But first let me give you two pieces of background regarding this story. This is a great example of why you shouldn't just grab a story out of the Bible without understanding the context in which that story is set.

Two things happened just prior to Jesus calming the sea. The first event took place at the very beginning of Jesus' public ministry. After He was baptized and filled with the Holy Spirit, the Scriptures say, Jesus was led into the Judean wilderness. There He spent 40 days fasting and praying. During that time, Jesus had an encounter with Satan in which He was tempted in powerful ways. I won't go into the various temptations now, but when the time of His temptation was over and He had successfully combatted Satan with the Word of God, the Bible says that Satan "withdrew until a more opportune time." Now, keep that phrase in mind.

In the second event, found in Mark chapter 1, Jesus was teaching in the synagogue in Capernaum when a demon-possessed man began shouting and hollering, disrupting the service. Jesus spoke deliberately and forcefully to that demon-possessed man, and the demons fled out of him. The man was set free.

We need to keep these two prior events in mind as we come to the story in Mark 4.

Jesus and His disciples were in the Capernaum area, on the north side of the Sea of Galilee. They were about to embark on a 13-mile trip across the sea, at night, in an open boat. The boat was probably about 18 feet long and made of huge timbers. More than likely, it was a rowboat of sorts.

We know why Jesus wanted to go to the other side: so He could have an encounter with another demon-possessed man.

> That day when evening came, he said to his disciples, "Let us go over to the other side." Leaving the crowd behind, they took him along, just as he was, in the boat. There were also other boats with him. A furious squall came up, and the waves broke over the boat, so that it was nearly swamped. (Mark 4:35-37)

Those of you who are familiar with the Sea of Galilee know that it sits 600 feet below sea level in something of a funnel, surrounded on three sides by very high mountains: the Golan Heights on the east, the Galilee mountains on the north, and Mount Arbel on the west. Mount Arbel towers over the city of Tiberias. When the wind blows over those mountains, it can cause great turbulence on the surface of the Sea of Galilee, as it funnels down through the Jordan Valley. Furious squalls can come up almost instantly.

That is what happened to Jesus' boat. A storm came up quickly, and the boat was nearly swamped.

> Jesus was in the stern, sleeping on a cushion. The disciples woke him and said to him, "Teacher, don't you care if we drown?" He got up, rebuked the wind and said to the waves, "Quiet! Be still!" (Mark 4:38-39)

Now, that's a civilized translation of what Jesus said. I grew up on the Broadman Hymnal, as many of you did. I grew up singing that nice little song, "The wind and the waves obey His will, peace be still, peace be still."

Well, Jesus wasn't speaking so gently, as that song would imply. When Jesus spoke to the storm, He used the exact same words He had used when He was spoke to the demon in Mark 1:25. He said the same thing to the demon in the man at the synagogue who was challenging Him. He told him to shut up and sit down. He told him to be quiet.

And that's exactly what He said to those waves: "Shut up and sit down!"

> He got up, rebuked the wind and said to the waves, "Quiet! Be still!" Then the wind died and it was completely calm. He said to his disciples, "Why are you so afraid? Do you still have no faith?" (Mark 4: 39-40)

His disciples must have looked at each other in disbelief. They were terrified—not by the storm; they were terrified by this man who was in the boat with them who could say to the wind, "Shut up!" and to the waves, "Sit down!" And nature obeyed Him.

> They were terrified and asked each other, "Who is this? Even the wind and the waves obey him." (Mark 4:41)

For the church to be the church today, we must understand who Jesus is. If we don't understand who Jesus is, we might as well go ahead and admit that we're just a social club—and not a very good social club at that. We're not nearly as good as the Rotary Club or the Kiwanis or the Lions or any of the others.

If you don't know who Jesus is—*the Lord of the church*—then you don't have any business being in church at all.

The true church is a group of people who function as a family—a family of people functioning under the lordship of Jesus Christ, both individually and corporately. The true church functions under the total lordship of Jesus Christ.

Now, as Christians, we say we believe that. But the fact is, when it comes right down to it, we're not really sure who Jesus is.

So, I ask you: who is Jesus? It's a good question. It's the very same question His disciples were asking when they said to one another, "Who is this? Even the wind and the waves obey him."

THE LAST ADAM

I won't go into a great deal of detail about this here. There are a lot of books written about who Jesus is—more than any room could ever contain. But allow me to give you just a tiny little summary. This is Paul speaking to the church at Rome regarding sin:

Nevertheless, death reigned from the time of Adam until the time of Moses [until the time that the law was given], even over those who did not sin by breaking a command, as did Adam, who was a pattern of the one to come. (Romans 5:14)

Notice, Adam was a pattern of the one to come. Okay then, who was Adam? He was more than the first man.

What did Adam have that made him unique above all other men? He had dominion over all things. He was placed in the Garden of Eden by God, who said, "I give you dominion over everything that is alive, even over nature itself. You, man, are placed here to tend this garden, and you have dominion over it. You have dominion over all the wild animals and beasts. They must do what you tell them to do. You have dominion over this garden and over all the natural aspects of this garden."

The one thing that characterized Adam over all others—and the one thing that he lost when he sinned—was dominion. When Adam sinned, he lost his dominion.

But the Scriptures also say Adam was a pattern of the one to come.

Let's move over to 1 Corinthians 15:22:

For as in Adam all die, so in Christ all will be made alive.

And then verse 45:

So it is written: "The first man Adam became a living being"; the last Adam, a life-giving spirit.

Again, who is Jesus? He is the last Adam. Jesus was placed here on Earth and given by God all those things that Adam had lost through sin, because Jesus was here without sin. What did

Jesus have that other men did not have, because He was without sin? He had dominion. He had dominion over nature and over all the things of nature, over all the underworld, over all the demons. Jesus had dominion over everything.

Adam was the pattern of one to come. Jesus came with the same dominion Adam had been given. And here in the Scripture He is called "the last Adam."

What we call a "miracle" when Jesus spoke to that rough water was Jesus exerting His godly nature, His dominion. And that dominion has now been returned to all His followers. In John 14:12, Jesus said this:

> I tell you the truth, anyone who has faith in me will do what
> I have been doing. He will do even greater things than these,
> because I am going to the Father.

What I'm doing is laying the groundwork to show you that the things Jesus did are still valid for today. They are for us as heirs to His kingdom. And if we unbelieving adults don't experience this reality because of our lack of faith, God will give pencils to Filipino boys, and He will give healings to Muslim children in the desert. Because they don't have enough sense not to believe. They simply accept it by faith.

"That preacher came through and said God will give me what I need, and I need a pencil. Please, Jesus, give me a pencil." And there it was. I saw it. There was not another pencil like it in all of Mindanao.

I also saw the child's head where the scab had come off during the night, and the child was healed—a Muslim child.

You may say, "Well, didn't that Muslim family accept Jesus?" No, they didn't accept Jesus.

"Why then did God heal?"

Because God lets His mercy fall on the just and the unjust. They qualified for healing simply because they asked God for it.

God doesn't just give healings to people who become Christians and stop dancing and smoking. No, God visits His mercy and His love upon all of His creatures.

How do you qualify for a healing? Simple: you ask Him for it.

Now, if you don't follow His healing and provision with a change in lifestyle, a change in your belief system, then you'll miss the other wonderful benefits of a relationship with God—all the better things He has for you. But God doesn't condition His love, His mercy, His grace, and His healing power. He doesn't put boundaries around it. No. God's love is for everyone.

Jesus came exhibiting dominion. He gave it to us as believers. But you can be certain the devil is continually trying to steal it from us. Satan will whisper, "It's okay if you believe it could only happen in the Philippines. It's okay if you believe it could only happen in the Sinai Desert. But it will not happen here, and it certainly won't happen to you."

That is a lie from the pit! Miracles and healings can and will happen *here*, and they can and will happen to *you*.

God is looking for a church that can be a Jesus church. A Jesus church is a church that believes what Jesus says and accepts what Jesus does. If you continue to sing, "He is Lord," you'd better be careful, if you're not willing for Him to actually be Lord of your life.

Jesus had harsh things to say and did harsh things to fig trees that only had leaves but no figs. If we're going to hold up a standard that says we're a Jesus church—or I'm a Jesus man, I'm a Jesus woman—then we should be prepared for Jesus to do His work through us. And if we block Him in any way, He will not be denied. He'll just pop up in the Philippines instead, and we will not see His glory.

We have dominion. It was given to us through the atonement of Jesus Christ. When He broke loose from that grave and was declared by angels and demons alike as "Lord of lords and King of kings," dominion was given to us.

At Pentecost, when the power of the Holy Spirit came, the promise that Jesus made to His disciples was fulfilled: "The same Spirit which lives in Me will now live in you."

We have it. It is ours. All we have to do is accept it, take it. What do I mean when I say, "Take it"?

I wrote a book with Corrie ten Boom some years ago called *Tramp for the Lord*. We had spent a lot of time together. She was a very wise Dutch woman who had suffered greatly at the hands of the Nazis, because she and her family had hidden Jewish people in Holland during World War II. She and her family ended up going into a concentration camp.

Because of what she went through during the war and her many years of following God, I trusted her judgment.

One day I was talking to Corrie about some missionary friends of mine who were Southern Baptists. They were in Indonesia and were going through a terrible, terrible situation. Their children were sick with all kinds of calamities. It seemed everything was coming down on them. And I said, "*Tante* Corrie, what do you think is going on here?"

And she said, "Oh, it's so simple. They have given all, but they haven't taken all."

"What do you mean, 'they haven't taken all'?"

She said, "They have not taken the dominion that Jesus gave them at Calvary. They've not taken it. They have not exerted the authority that is theirs over the devil who would kill and destroy, and they have caved in under satanic pressure."

BACK TO SCHOOL

Several years ago, I was invited to go back and speak at my alma mater, Mercer University in Macon, Georgia. It's the Baptist college I graduated from in the early 1950s. I had all but forgotten about the school, even though I had been president of my fraternity and head of this and head of that. After graduation, I'd get a letter once in a while from the alumni association asking for money, but I never would send any. I just thought that was a phase of my life that I had passed through. I had moved on, not really wanting to look back.

Then I got a letter from the vice president of the university asking me to come and speak at their weekly chapel service. I thought, *I wonder if they know who they're asking? I'm not even a Baptist anymore.* I had been, but our church had been unseated by our local association. They'd told us to "please leave and not cause any trouble." Well, we left, but the whole process caused trouble. Just our presence in the community was a continual agitation to the other Baptist churches.

I didn't know what to do about that. I had struggled with it, and I was heartbroken over it. But it was a fact just the same.

So, I couldn't understand why I, a renegade Baptist, would be invited to speak at this Georgia Baptist school. I didn't understand—as least not until I found out that they frequently invited all kinds of weird people to come in and speak at their chapel. And I was one of those weird people. Unbeknownst to me, Mercer University had developed something of a liberal streak. In fact, my chapel invitation was sandwiched between the invitations of Bernadette Devlin, who was an Irish terrorist with the IRA, and Jane Fonda.

Anyway, I accepted. The invitation was there, and I thought I might like to go back and see my old campus.

The next Sunday at church I told the congregation what I was going to do, and I asked them to pray for me. After the service a lady came up to me and asked, "Do you know what you're going to say when you get there?"

I said, "No, but I'm going to work on it tonight and on the plane tomorrow."

She said, "Well, I have a word from the Lord for you. God says that you are to give no thought to what you are to say. He will put words in your mouth when you stand to speak."

I couldn't help but grimace. "Well, thanks a lot. That's just what I need to hear right now. I'm going to go back and speak at my alma mater for the very first time, and God says don't make any preparation for what I'm going to say. That's just great."

She smiled and said, "That's what God told me."

I was kind of jittery about the whole thing to begin with. I remembered how we had treated some of our chapel speakers when I was a student there. I mean, we treated them with the utmost disrespect. We would read newspapers while they were speaking and made loud remarks and even obscene gestures.

I remembered when Louie D. Newton came to speak. Dr. Newton was pastor of Druid Hills Baptist Church in Atlanta, Georgia, and former president of the Southern Baptist Convention. Old Dr. Newton had come down from Atlanta to speak in Macon at the great Mercer University chapel service, and the students could not have cared less who he was. They made fun of him something awful. He had this exaggerated Georgia preacher drawl when he spoke, and when he stood up and said, "Hello, Georgia Baptists," we all went, "Boo!"

It was terrible. I was sitting out there, booing along with all the rest of them. To us, this was just another preacher in another chapel service that we were going to have to sit through. Chapel was required back then, and everybody had to be there. But they couldn't control how we handled ourselves.

I remembered that day and I thought, *Now I've got to go speak before this student body, and God has said, "Give no thought to what you're going to say. I'll put words in your mouth."*

Have you ever tried to go speak anywhere and not give thought to what you're going to say? It's hard. And now I had this word from God—at least it seemed to be from God.

I mulled it over in my mind all that night and the next day as I flew to Macon. I was going to spend the night in my old dormitory on the campus, and then I was going to speak at the 10 a.m. chapel service the next morning.

I kept saying, "God, if You'll just give me the first sentence . . ." But, no. Nothing.

Don't write anything down and don't think about it. Think about anything else. Think about green-eyed monkeys, about bananas, about the moon, about the weather. Think about anything else. God will put words in my mouth.

I got up that morning and walked over to the chapel, and it was packed. The entire university administration was there, the faculty was there, and the whole student body was present. They were cut from the same old cloth that I had been. They carried newspapers and books and had their feet propped up on the backs of the pews. They could not have cared less.

It was Tuesday morning required chapel at Mercer University. And I was on the platform.

As soon as the doors closed, the vice president introduced me. He reminded everyone that they were having a series of speakers who'd had different kinds of spiritual experiences. And today they had an author from Florida, who, by the way, was a graduate of their school.

Then it was my turn. I had been sitting on the platform with the deans and administrators, thinking about all the things I had to do when I got back home to Florida, when I suddenly realized my name had been called, and I had to get up and speak. And I had no idea what I was going to say.

The vice president turned to me and said, "You're up."

I got up slowly, walked over to the microphone, opened my mouth—and out of my mouth came the most absurdly ridiculous statement. If I had dreamed for 100 years of the one thing I did not want to say, that was what I said.

I opened my mouth and said, "I'm a Southern Baptist pastor who's been fired from two churches, and I speak in tongues."

Oh, dear God. You didn't just do that to me, did you?

I watched all the newspapers come down. The books closed. The administrators sat up on the edge of their seats. Even the faculty on the front row sat up on the edge of their seats. Everybody, it seemed, was waiting to hear what I had to say next.

Now what, Lord? And God said, "Now, Jamie, you're on your own."

I thought, *Well I've already made a total fool of myself. I might as well keep going.*

So, for the next 45 minutes I told them my story. I told them how I had once been a student at Mercer, later went on to seminary, and then became a Baptist pastor at a church not too far from there in Greenwood, South Carolina. And the whole time I was empty.

Then I had an experience with the Holy Spirit.

I told them about that and about all the miracles I had witnessed, and about how the Word of God had gone from being just words in a book to a living object within my heart. I told them about the joy and the adventure and the riskiness of living a Spirit-led life. "It's risky living," I told them, "to give yourself fully over to Jesus Christ. It's risky from a human standpoint. But it's absolutely necessary if you want to receive everything God has for you."

Finally, I finished and sat down. The vice president who had introduced me just sat there, staring at me. Nobody moved. The place was totally quiet. Everybody's eyes were glued on me. I was finished, and I didn't know what to do next.

I knew I had a plane to catch. A friend of mine was going to meet me outside and take me to the airport. I thought, *Surely someone will dismiss this thing.* I mean, we had finished about five minutes ahead of the scheduled dismissal. *Certainly we're not going to just sit here in silence for five minutes.*

It was over, but still nobody moved.

So, I got up and started down the aisle. I got to about the third row of pews when a young student stood up, moved out of his seat, and walked up directly in front of me, blocking my way.

"Do you believe everything you just said?" he asked.

I said, "Son, it sounded so foolish that if I didn't believe it, I ought to be shot. Yes, I believe everything I just said."

I looked at him closely. He was six feet tall and weighed about 90 pounds. The hair on his head had fallen out in great patches. His skin was yellow, his face sunken.

"I'm dying of leukemia," he said. "My older brother died last year of the same thing. I was doing chemotherapy, but the doctors said it won't do any good at this point, and they've stopped it. They said I'll be dead before the school year is out. Do you believe God can heal me?"

I said, "Yes, sir, I do."

Everybody was sitting there watching us as we had this conversation in the aisle. Then he said, "Will you pray for me?"

"Yes, I'll pray for you."

He said, "Now?"

I said, "Now." And I reached out to put my hands on him to pray. But before I even touched him, he collapsed in the aisle. For a moment I thought he was dead. He had barely been able to stand up before, and now he had just crumbled.

A couple of his friends who'd been sitting next to him immediately got down on the floor beside him. I stood there and watched for a minute as they helped him back up to his feet. He was okay, so I walked on around them and out the door.

My buddy who was going to take me back to the airport had enough good sense to stay outside. I caught the plane and went back to Florida.

I never did hear anything from anybody at Mercer after that service. Nobody ever said anything to me. They didn't write. They didn't call. They didn't even pay for my expenses, as they had promised. And that was fine. I didn't want to hear from them, and I was delighted to pay my own way. I didn't want to think any more about that situation. It was as though it had never taken place.

Three years later, on a Saturday night, I was speaking at a small Full Gospel Businessmen's gathering in Cocoa, Florida, about 15 miles north of where I live. We were meeting at a little restaurant, and there were about 40 people present. For whatever reason, I felt led to tell the story about going up to speak at Mercer.

I was about to move into the main point of my message when a man and woman I had never seen before, sitting at a table in the back, stood to their feet and interrupted me. The man said, "May I say something?"

I said, "Sure. Strange things have happened to me before. Nothing could be any stranger than what I've already been through. So go ahead and say whatever you want to."

Immediately his voice choked up. "We're from Athens, Georgia," he said. "We are in Florida vacationing, and we read in the newspaper that you were going to be speaking at this meeting. So, my wife and I decided to drive over from our hotel in Orlando to see you personally. I had no idea you were going to tell that story."

He paused, his voice cracking a little. Then he said, "That boy is my son. He is totally healed. He's now a second-year med student at the University of Georgia in Athens."

The room erupted in cheers and hallelujahs!

I've since heard from the young man. He completed his medical degree and to date, as far as I know, he continues to function in good health.

Dominion.

PRAY WITH THE SPIRIT

You don't have to know how to pray, you just have to be willing to do it—that's all. How do you pray? I don't know how you pray, other than to pray like Jesus prayed. How did Jesus pray? He prayed in many different ways. He put spit on people. He put mud in their eyes. He touched them. He pushed them away.

However the Spirit leads you to pray, that's how you pray.

How you pray is totally unimportant. The important thing is that you let God take control of your life and manifest Himself here on Earth, so that Jesus can be glorified.

Miracles are not for the sake of the miracle. Miracles are for the sake of glorifying God—because God loves hurting people. That's all.

When a church becomes a miracle church, people will drive hundreds of miles to be there for the services, either because they're curious and they want to see somebody healed, or because they're hurting and they want to be healed themselves. Where else can they go?

What do you do when you're in extremis, and everybody else has given up on you? What do you do when your life falls apart? What do you do when you're at the end of your rope, you're in despair, and you see no hope at all? You go to where God's people are. Jesus is there. And Jesus is the same today as He was yesterday. He will work through His church, and He will heal.

I have never known a church anywhere in the world that did not grow when Jesus was being glorified and His miracles were happening. There are so many programs on church growth available to us. I'll tell you something about church growth: dump the programs. Dump them all. There is one thing that will draw people to a church, and that's the presence of the living Lord. His presence will draw people.

I don't want to say you shouldn't have programs. But if you don't have figs on your tree, and all you've got are leaves, you're going to be hurt. And eventually you'll wind up without figs *or* leaves.

IN DUE TIME

Let me tell you one more story. I had spoken at a little meeting in Titusville, Florida. My friend Peter Lord, who is pastor at Park Avenue Baptist Church in Titusville, arranged this for me. It was a group of businessmen, and I just shared a little of my personal testimony.

I'm an extremely simple guy. I'm not a great Bible expositor. I love and understand the Bible, but that's not my method of teaching. Others are good at that, and I appreciate it, but I'm a storyteller.

So, I shared a few things out of my life. When I'd finished speaking, a man came up to me and said, "I'm pastor of the Presbyterian church here in Titusville. Would you be willing to come speak in my church?" Then he added, "We want what you have."

I looked at him as kindly as I could and said, "No. You don't want what I have. Because I'll tell you what I bring with me. I bring trouble. If I come into your church cold, with no explanation, I will bring trouble. You've heard me today, and you're excited about the presence of Jesus and the power of the Holy Spirit and the supernatural power of a miracle-working God. But if I go to your congregation and begin to talk about all that, I'm going to split your church wide open."

"So how can we get this?" he asked.

"I'll tell you what I'll do. You're a Presbyterian church, so you've got elders in the church. I will meet with your elders, and I will share with them. If they are willing to cooperate with me, then we'll do it as a team, together."

"That sounds like wisdom," he said. "That's a fair assessment."

A month later, he called me on the phone. "I've got a meeting set up with my elders. Some are outgoing elders and others are incoming elders. It's a group of about 12 men. Will you come and meet with us?"

"Absolutely. I'll be there," I said.

So, I drove up on a Tuesday night from Melbourne to Titusville, about 45 minutes. I went into the Sunday school classroom where they were meeting. Everyone was sitting in a circle in tiny kiddie chairs. As I entered, they each stood up and introduced themselves.

It was a rather astute group of people. That particular area on the east coast of Florida is full of people who work in the aerospace industry. It's where NASA's Kennedy Space Center is located, as well as Cape Canaveral Air Force Station. The group of elders sitting in the little circle included a couple of aerospace engineers, a couple of physicists, a doctor, and the guy who was in charge of launch activities for NASA.

There are some really neat people who are Presbyterians!

They sat around talking Presbyterian-talk for a while, and then it was my turn. After the pastor introduced me, I began to share.

"Now fellows, your pastor asked me to do this. He asked me to come up here to speak to your church. But first I wanted a chance to talk with you. Let me tell you who I am, what has happened to me, and where I'm coming from."

I took about 30 minutes and shared with them who I was. When I finished, we just sat there looking at each other. Apparently, they had never heard anything like that before—ever.

"Well, that's it," I said. "I'm going to leave so you guys can talk about this some more. But I'm not coming back unless you fellows are in total agreement."

As I started to leave, one of the men, an aerospace engineer at NASA, said, "I've got to say something. I've been sitting on this uncomfortable little chair all night, and my back is killing me. I was in a car accident a couple of weeks ago, and I got whiplash. I can hardly stand the pain. It's been tough sitting on this little chair. It has just ruined me tonight. I thought I was going to have to get up and leave, I hurt so bad."

And then he said, "Do you believe God can heal me?"

"Sure," I said. "That's what this is all about. It's the reason I'm here. I believe God can heal you."

"Would you pray for me?"

"No," I said.

"Why not?"

"Because I'm in a group of church elders, and the Scriptures are very specific about what is to happen when elders are present. 'If there is anybody sick, let him call for the elders of the church, and they'll anoint with oil, and the prayer of faith will raise him up.' These other elders are the ones who should pray for you."

One of the guys said, "We don't know how to pray for him. We've never prayed for anybody like this."

"Well," I said, "you anoint him with oil and pray for him."

"We don't have any oil."

"Hey," another man said. "The kitchen's back there. I'll bet there's some oil in the kitchen. I'll go get some. You guys wait here."

He turned and went through the door to the little kitchen. And we waited and waited and waited. I thought, *Oh boy, that guy's gone home. He went out the back door and left us in here.*

Just about that time, he pushed the door open. In his hand he held a small saucer. "I couldn't find any oil," he said, "but I found some butter in the refrigerator. I had to melt it in the microwave. That's why I took so long."

I said to the guy with the hurting back, "You stand here in the middle of this circle. We're going to gather around you and anoint you with oil."

So, we all stood around him in a circle. These folks had never done anything like this in their lives. They had been in church for decades, but nothing like this had ever happened. I took the saucer of melted butter and passed it around. We each stuck a finger in it as it passed.

"Now," I said, "put the oil on him."

"Where?" someone asked.

"Well, it doesn't matter, really. Perhaps his forehead. Or just wipe it on him someplace."

So here were all these Presbyterian elders—all these physicists and engineers and rocket scientists—standing around this guy, wiping butter all over him. It was crazy—absolutely wild! The pastor just stood there, shaking his head.

"What do we do next?" they asked.

"Now we pray."

But before I had a chance to speak a prayer, I heard one of the guys begin to cry. He was sobbing. Then the man next to him began to cry. And suddenly God's presence was felt, and we all started to cry. The only person not crying was the guy standing in the middle. Instead, he was twisting from side to side and bending forward and backward.

"Guys, guys!" he said. "I'm okay. I feel good. My back doesn't hurt anymore. I think I'm healed!"

The men began crying for joy and laughing and hugging each other. Soon everyone had melted butter all over their hands and faces and suit jackets.

I came back a month later, and we had a couple of glorious meetings with the whole congregation. We had healings every night. People came forward to accept Jesus for the first time, and others received the baptism in the Holy Spirit. The elders came forward and anointed people with oil. They had the real stuff by then.

WE ARE THE CHURCH

Let me tell you what I learned from that entire experience: God doesn't give a hoot about your image. God looks at the heart. God is looking for men and women who want to glorify Him and are willing to be fools for Jesus' sake to do it. He is looking for people who forget about their self-image, who forget about what other people are thinking about them, and step out in faith to glorify God for His sake.

If we do that, then we will have churches full of people who are Spirit-filled and Spirit-led. If we are willing to reach out and lay hands on the sick ourselves, we won't need to bring in the big healing ministries, because healing will be happening in our churches. It will be happening when we go to each other's houses and anoint each other with oil and pray with one another.

Healings will happen in the hospitals, and you won't even have to call for the pastor or the visitation team. When they get there, the healing will have already taken place, because you've been there and you've taken the dominion that Jesus Christ has given to you. You will be the one who goes in, and you will be the one who says, "In the name of Jesus."

You can say to the turmoil and the storms in life, "Sit down and shut up." And they'll stop. You can speak to the weather and to nature itself. No evil thing will befall you or your family or your friends or those around you—all because of the authority and the dominion that God has given to you through Jesus Christ.

That's the church, people. That's the family of God functioning under the lordship of Jesus Christ. Everything else we do is secondary to that.

We come together to celebrate. We come together to worship. We come together to train. We come together to study the Bible. We come together for social functions. We come together to eat. All that is wonderful and good and excellent. But the most important thing is that we go out into this world as Jesus people. That's what God is looking for. That's what He's waiting for from each of you.

Are you okay with that?

I understand this may upset some folks. Why? Because it's true, and the truth always upsets people. That's what this book we call the Bible will do. It's filled with this stuff! And we are people of the Bible.

That's what it's all about. The lordship of Jesus Christ means *the actual lordship of Jesus Christ* over us—over everything.

We'd be amiss if we didn't pray for those around us. We should do that. Families are supposed to pray for each other. We're supposed to pray for ourselves, our spouse, our kids. We are commanded to pray for the people God has put in our lives.

When the church meets together, we should let the leadership in the church—those who occupy the eldership roles—pray for us. If there's anybody who's sick among you, the Bible says, let the elders anoint him with oil, and trust God to do the healing.

God wants His church to be a place of healing. He wants the word to go out that people can come to the church and be healed. Bring your sick, bring your diseased, bring those that the world says are terminal. Bring your AIDS patients, bring your drug addicts. Bring those whose hearts are broken and destroyed.

Jesus said, "I came for the sick, not for the well. They're the ones who need the Physician." When you go out, bring the sick and the hurting back with you, and Jesus will touch them. He will touch them through the body called the church. And when that happens, those people will become the best evangelists your church will ever have.

You get one man who was sick and is healed, and he'll go walking and leaping through every temple in your community.

All you need to do is trust. It's God who heals.

Who has the gift of healing? The one who has the gift of healing is the one who receives the healing. If you are sick and you are healed, then you have just received the gift of healing. The Holy Spirit has given it to you. The rest of us just function in faith, that's all.

So, if you're sick, call upon the church to pray for you. If you're not sick, then you have the great honor and privilege to pray for those who are. That is the church functioning as it was intended to function—with authority and dominion.

CHAPTER 4

THE CRY OF THE WILD GOOSE

Somebody asked me if I knew where I was going with all these things I've been telling you. To answer simply: yes, I do know where I am going.

I have been bringing you deliberately through various stages of my own personal experience with being led by the Spirit of God. In fact, as I've thought about it, I have come to the conclusion that just about everything we do in life happens in stages—and that includes our spiritual life, our walk with the Lord, our supernatural experiences with a loving God, as the Holy Spirit guides us on an ever-wondrous walk through life.

You don't ever get to where you want to go instantly. That is, unless you want a hamburger. Then you can just drive your car up to the box and talk to it. But for anything that is really worthwhile, anything that's nutritious, anything that's lasting, you have to go through various steps and stages to get there. You have to struggle with it. You don't get there instantly, especially if you are steeped in a tradition that says, "You can't go there," or you're caught in a cycle of sin that has blinded you from the real goals God has for you. Getting where God wants you to be takes a while. It takes time, and it takes patience.

What I have been doing is laying the groundwork for an understanding of the concept I stated at the beginning: that it really is possible for the deep desires of your heart to come to pass. It is possible for your dreams to come true.

Søren Kierkegaard, the 19th century Danish theologian, was something of an existentialist. Actually, he was more than just a dry intellectual, as many classify him. He was also a great writer of short stories.

Years ago, Kierkegaard wrote a short story about a flock of geese that lived in a barnyard in Denmark. Apparently, these geese understood congregational rule, and they had selected a leader—a preaching goose—who, every week on Sunday morning, would "honk" his flock together into the barnyard. Then the preacher goose would climb up on the top rail of the pulpit-platform and preach to the gathered goose congregation about the glories of Goose-dom.

How wonderful it was that they had a Creator who had a dream for them, he would say. And now they were fulfilling this dream. They, the geese, were different from all the other creatures in the barnyard. They should be thanking and praising their Goose God that they weren't hens or ducks, or, even worse, turkeys. No, they were geese, and they were special.

On occasion, while the preaching goose was expounding upon the glories of Goose-dom, the barnyard geese would look up. High above, they would see a flock of wild geese flying in V-formation. They were moving south at perhaps 90 or 100 miles an hour at an altitude of 8,000 feet, flying from Norway to Austria. Sometimes the barnyard geese would observe the flying geese heading back in the opposite direction, moving north, their migration over for the season.

Whenever the flying geese appeared in the skies, the barnyard geese would grow quiet. They would cock their ears and listen for the leading wild goose to call from above. And the preaching goose would shout, "That's who we are! We are not destined for this barnyard. One day, we are going to cross Jordan's icy waters, and we will fly with them. That's who we are meant to be."

The barnyard geese would all go, "Honk, honk, honk," which is the goose equivalent to "Amen, preacher!" Then they would get "people-bumps" up and down their backs and feel good about who they were as they watched the wild geese disappear out of sight.

On those occasions when they would hear the cry of the wild geese as they flew by on their way to destiny, the grounded geese would turn and look at each other and give each other the right wing of fellowship. What a marvelous thing to observe! Then the preaching goose would come down off the rail, and they'd all go back into the barn to eat corn, grow fat, and wait for Christmas to come.

A SPIRIT OF ADVENTURE

I think about Kierkegaard's story as I consider all the times I have heard the cry of the wild goose in my own heart.

You see, I believe there is built into every one of us, put there by God, a spirit of adventure. I believe that we are, by nature, adventurous people. We are different. There is no other creature on the face of the earth that has the spirit of adventure we humans do. Animals don't have it. Fowls don't have it. Plants don't have it. Only mankind has the spirit of adventure. "Let's go do it!" "Let's see if we can make it work!" "Let's try it out!" That's the marvelous spirit of adventure we have as human beings.

In the spiritual realm, we call it faith. It's that willingness to step out into an impossible situation and trust God to do something special in our lives.

The problem is, even though we have that spirit of adventure, we seldom act on it. Instead, we are satisfied to return to the barn and eat corn.

We are like the spies that Moses sent into the Promised Land who saw the walled cities and the giants of Anak. Suddenly we shrink in size, and the obstacles grow in size. We become like grasshoppers in our own sight. We see giants and we retreat, saying, "It can't be done. The obstacles are too great. I'll never become who God wants me to be. I just can't make it."

I have a psychologist friend who says there are three things necessary for personal fulfillment. The first is a sense of personal worth. Who am I? Until that is settled and you know who you are, you will always be frustrated.

The second thing needed for personal fulfillment is a sense of calling. What am I to do? You need to know you have a special place in this world. It's not just about who you are; it's about what your role is in life. Until you are in that role—or at least heading toward it—you are going to remain frustrated.

The third thing that is necessary for fulfillment is a dream. There must be something that's bigger than you are, something that beckons you to move forward.

The cry of the wild goose says you are not meant for the mud and the manure of the barnyard. You're meant to fly, not just waddle around. You are meant for clean air, a destiny, a destination, a dream, a higher goal. That's who you really are.

WHAT IS SALVATION?

What is your definition of salvation? I grew up with various definitions. Most of them came from the little four-page tracts my mother used to give to me. But let me offer you a definition that I think is biblical: Salvation is becoming who God intends for you to be.

There's a difference between conversion and salvation, and I hope you understand that. I don't want to get too deep into theology here, but there is a difference between the two.

Conversion is an experience. It happens once. Salvation, however, is a process that starts with conversion and continues on for the rest of your life on Earth—and maybe even in heaven. Will there be spiritual growth on the other side? We don't know for sure. But we do know that unless there is spiritual growth here on Earth, we are not being saved. Salvation is a process.

Salvation can never be spoken of in the past tense. We use the wrong terminology when we say, "I was saved." No, you weren't saved; you are *being* saved. It's a continuing process that goes on and on and on.

You can say, "I was converted." You moved from death to life, from darkness into light. That's an experience. It happened. It's called the "new birth," and it only takes place once. But the moment the new birth takes place, you begin to grow. And that's what salvation is.

There are many steps in the salvation process—steps you have to go through to grow and to get where God wants you to be. He has a plan for your life, and that plan involves taking steps. That's why we call the Christian life a "walk."

There's just enough Calvinism in me to believe that God has ordained something good for everyone who has been called according to His purpose. It has been preordained. It's just for you. He knows your name. He has a slot picked out for you, and He has something wonderful planned for your life. He has put echoes in your heart of what that is. You sense it. You know it. You may get it mixed up with material things, but deep down inside, you know that God has something special just for you. It's your dream, your desire, your calling.

The older I grow, the more important that "something special" becomes to me. I'm concerned about what I'm supposed to do with the productive years I have left in my life. I believe that everything up until this point has been training for what is to come next. As I have grown older, my dreams have actually gotten bigger and wider—not narrower, as I see happening to too many elderly people.

I believe there is a difference between getting older and getting old. In fact, I believe it is possible to grow older without getting old at the same time.

My mother is old, and her entire world has narrowed down to just the bed she is lying in. Her primary concern in her nursing home is whether there is a wrinkle in the sheet under her back. That wrinkle is as big as any mountain or obstacle you could ever encounter, if it's annoying you and you can't turn over. To her, that pesky wrinkle in her sheet is a pretty big thing.

Yet, I hear God saying, "I don't want My people to be like that." God doesn't want my mother to be that way. I don't think He wants any of us to go out that way. I think there are better ways for us to leave this world. Wouldn't it be great if we could all go out like old Isaac? Call your children in, bless them, pull the covers up, then go on to live in eternity with God? Isn't that the way it ought to happen? *Poof!* Just like that, and you're with your Father in heaven.

I think God wants us to die healthy. I don't think God wants us to die sick. I don't think He wants us to go out with horrible diseases. I think He wants us to be healthy right up until the time we die.

Now, most of us won't get to do that, because we don't cooperate with God in our younger years, when we have opportunities to cooperate with Him. In order to be healthy into old age, you need to start when you are 15, or maybe 25. There's a whole host of things you can do—or not do—to cooperate with the Lord. You can't go to McDonald's every day for dinner, for example. But I'll not get into all of that.

My concern is about where I'm supposed to be going and what I'm supposed to be doing with my life in the years I have ahead of me. We should all be concerned. And our dreams should be enlarging and increasing as we grow older.

Carl Jung, the Swiss psychiatrist, said the tragedy of life is that we usually spend the entire first half establishing our outer identity. We don't even begin to touch our inner identity until we have passed middle age. Only then do we begin to get concerned about who we are. Up until then, we are consumed with what we are supposed to do.

If we would train ourselves to reverse that process, we could say of our latter years, as Elizabeth Barrett Browning poetically wrote, "The best is yet to be."

If we, as Christians, could spend our early years making a determination about who we are in Christ—getting our status with God correct, getting our status with each other correct, getting our status with our purpose on Earth correct—then God would make the last years of our lives truly productive, engaging, eventful, and fulfilling.

But most of us spend all our energy in those early years trying to make money so we can retire. We are more interested in making money than establishing a relationship with God. And because of that, when we grow old, our minds are already set and programmed, so that all we think about are material things and serving ourselves.

I've been thinking about the calls on my life. Who am I? What am I to do? What are my desires? What are my dreams?

Perhaps you've been asking yourself these questions, too. I want to tell you a couple of stories that I believe can help you find your answers.

DREAM BIG

Walt Disney, who bought up half of Florida, it seems, back in the 1970s, grew up in Ohio. His brother, Roy, who owns the other half of Florida, is now the brains behind all the Disney enterprises.

I heard Roy tell this story about Walt several years ago. He said that when Walt was growing up, he went to 5th grade in a one-room schoolhouse. All the other grades were with him in the same room.

One day Walt's teacher gave the students an art assignment. They were asked to draw things in nature—trees, grass, flowers, bushes, stars, clouds, and other things like that. So, all the kids went to work. They had their construction paper and their crayons, and they were all working on the art project. As the teacher was walking up and down the aisles, she got to where the little Disney boy was sitting. She leaned over and looked at his paper. Then she reached down and picked it up.

"Now Walter," she said, "that's really nice. Those are beautiful flowers. But Walter, don't you know? Flowers don't have faces on them."

Walt Disney—just a little guy sitting at his desk in a one-room schoolhouse—looked up at his teacher and said, "Oh, but teacher! Mine do."

And they did. Not only did Walt Disney's flowers have faces, but his elephants could fly, and his crickets could talk, and the mouse he drew changed the world—all because a little kid had a dream, and he wouldn't let his teachers or anybody else put out the fire of that dream.

I believe God has placed dreams in each one of us. They're ours. God has put them in us.

I've got a little note in the front of my Bible. I wrote it to myself a number of years ago. It says, "Jamie, don't let the world, or the church, fashion you into its mold."

In other words, be a free agent, my brother, my sister! Learn what it's like to walk before God in freedom. Learn what it's like to walk individually before God. Don't become part of the pack and just go along with everyone else. Be an individual. Be unique. Hear from God yourself, and don't ever allow yourself to be trapped into lockstep with the world.

If you hear from God correctly, and if your brother hears from God correctly, you will walk in unison together. You'll never be out there wandering around alone, doing your own thing, if you are hearing from God correctly. But God will speak to each one of us individually, and He will tell us essentially the same things, but our individual approaches will be different.

The problem is that we don't really believe God will speak to us and come through for us. We're afraid to flap our wings and fly when we hear the cry of the wild goose. Why? Because we're afraid we can't fly, regardless of what God has said.

What if you sit on top of the rail of the fence and flap your wings and go "honk, honk, honk" and step off—and fall nose-down into the mud? It is a risk you run. But you will never know whether you can fly or not if you don't trust God, flap your wings, and take a step of faith. You will never know whether the prayer of faith will heal the sick if you don't lay hands on others and pray. You will never know whether God can work a miracle through you unless you are willing to trust Him for a miracle.

If you are not willing to try, miracles will always be something you read about but never experience for yourself. Miracles will always be for those other geese—the ones flying overhead following the call of God. They will never be for you.

Your dreams can be fulfilled. Those deep spiritual dreams that God has purposefully and intentionally planted in you can be fulfilled. But they will only be fulfilled if you do something about it. You will have to step out. You will have to flap your wings. You will have to run the risk of failure.

KEEP FLYING

That is especially difficult for those in leadership. When folks in leadership fail, they fail in public, in front of everybody. And sometimes God will allow leaders to fail deliberately, as a test to see what kind of stuff they are made of. God wants to see if we will climb back up on the fencepost, wipe the mud off our feathers, and try to fly again.

Robert Frost wrote this in his poem, *The Road Not Taken*:

I shall be telling this with a sigh
Somewhere ages and ages hence:
Two roads diverged in a wood, and I,
I took the one less traveled by,
And that has made all the difference.

God is looking for men and women who are willing to take the road "less traveled by"—those who will enter at the narrow gate while the majority takes the broad way; those who will say, "I will run the risk of failure. I will trust God."

Years ago, I clipped out and pasted in the front of my Bible a prayer that A.W. Tozer wrote for his own ordination service. Tozer was a marvelous preacher from another generation, and his grandson is one of my favorite people. The prayer is rich and profound:

Lord Jesus, I come to thee for spiritual preparation. Lay thy hand upon me. Anoint me with the oil of the New Testament prophet. Forbid that I should become a religious scribe and thus lose my prophetic calling. Save me from the curse that lies dark across the face of the modern clergy, the curse of compromise, of imitation, of professionalism. Save me from the error of judging a church by its size, its popularity, or the amount of its yearly offering. Let me never become a slave to crowds. Heal my soul of carnal ambition and deliver me from the itch for publicity. Deliver me from over-eating and late-sleeping. Teach me self-discipline, that I may be a good soldier of Jesus Christ.

That's powerful stuff! No wonder God used A.W. Tozer to impact so many for Christ in his own generation and beyond.

THE CALL OF GOD

Each one of us has a fire in our bones. Jeremiah struggled with this fact. Jeremiah was a lonely Old Testament prophet who was called by God to speak out against governments and religious institutions. He was called by God when nobody else was called. In his generation, he was the only voice crying out. He was literally a voice in the wilderness.

Nobody liked what he had to say. He was stoned. Mud was slung at him. He stayed miserable most of his life, until he finally reached the place where he could stand it no longer. He marched into God's enlistment office, threw his papers on the table, and said, "I resign. I will not reenlist again. I am through."

Oh Lord, you deceived me, and I was deceived; you overpowered me and prevailed. I am ridiculed all day long; everyone mocks me. Whenever I speak, I cry out proclaiming violence and destruction. So the word of the Lord has brought me insult and reproach all day long. (Jeremiah 20:7-8)

Jeremiah was saying, "God, You are bigger than I am, and it's not fair. You pushed me around and kicked me, and I'm too weak to resist. You bullied me into this thing. It's not my fault. It's Your fault, God. I've been cut up, battered, stoned, and bruised, and it's all Your fault."

Then suddenly Jeremiah begins to recollect:

But if I say, "I will not mention him or speak any more in his name," his word is in my heart like a burning fire, a fire shut up in my bones. I am weary of holding it in, indeed, I cannot. (Jeremiah 20:9)

When God has a call on your life, even though you get beat up and bullied because of it, you can't go back. You can't renounce the call—not if it is really from God. You can't do it. It burns inside of you like a fire in your bones. It's there. You can't shake it. You can't get rid of it. You can't flee from it. There's nothing you can do to make God's call go away, because God has placed it there inside of you. That's that spirit of adventure. Those are the dreams God has implanted in you. They are now a part of you, and you can't ignore them.

God Himself has placed inside of you the desire of your heart. It's there—inside each one of you. But, you see, it is basically a spiritual desire. I talk to people and ask, "What's your dream in life?" They say, "Make a million dollars before I'm 40." That's not a dream. That's a carnal ambition. It won't last. All it will do is buy you an expensive casket.

That's not an ample dream. That's not a worthy dream. That is not a dream placed in your heart by God.

The only dreams that are worthy, the only dreams that are ample, are those that will live on beyond you. I'm not talking about having your name on the front door of a great building or on a plaque behind a pew in the church. That's only a memorial. I'm talking about something that moves on and lives eternally, something that can only happen when your dream is an investment in the kingdom. That's all. Only when your life and your dream are invested in the kingdom of God is there anything that goes beyond this earthly life. Those are the only dreams that are worthy. And the potential for such a dream—a lasting dream—is inside of every one of us.

MADE TO WORSHIP

Man is meant to worship. But we have been curtailed in our worship by our traditions, by our fears, by our lack of an adventurous spirit. We're concerned about what somebody else will say about us, what they will think of us.

The psalmist said, "Let everything that is within me praise the Lord." What is within you? All the cells of your body, that's what! With all the desires God has placed within you, I don't think He intends for you to sit still on a bench, holding a 75-year-old hymnbook in front of you, and call that worship. That's singing a hymn. It's okay. But is it really worship? Are you singing from your heart, or are you just mouthing words?

I'm not saying you can't worship by singing ancient hymns. I love many of them, and occasionally we sing them in my church. But true worship demands that everything within you praise the Lord.

When you move into true worship, you have to struggle to hold your body still. All the cells in your body want to go aerobic. They want to move, raise their hands, clap, bow down, even dance before the Lord like David did.

That doesn't mean you jump up and down all the time, or even most of the time. It simply means that inside of you something is happening, something is moving, and you are moving, because you are worshiping the living God, Creator of the universe.

If you are willing to let go, true worship will happen. It's there inside of you. You're going to have to shout out to the Lord and sing His praises, at least once in a while. You can't contain it forever. It's a fire in your bones. If you elect to keep your mouth shut, believe me, the rocks will cry out instead.

I get angry sometimes when I think about the tradition I was raised in—a tradition that said I wasn't allowed to physically express my love for God. I couldn't clap my hands in church. That was not dignified.

Suggesting a set of drums in church was like asking to introduce Satan's very own instrument into the sanctuary.

"Next you'll be wanting us to get mixed up with those demonic guitars," people objected. "Honky-tonk music off the highway would surely follow. Shame on you for considering it!"

True worship is composed of three parts. They are the same three parts that most music is composed of. First, there is rhythm. God intends for you to be filled with rhythm. Either you tap your foot, or you clap your hands, or you jump up and down, or you do something else to your liking. But you've got to get some kind of beat going. The church today needs to get a beat going. Beat—rhythm—is fine. That's the part of worship that appeals to the physical aspect of our body.

Second, there is melody. We sometimes call it "soul music." Humans are part soul, too, as well as body. I have to have something melodic inside of me. I need a line to sing to, a verse to respond to, a linear succession of musical tones to hum along with.

The third element is harmony. This is the part I believe God is most like—Father, Son, and Holy Spirit, all singing together in three-part harmony. No one is fussing over who gets the lead. Everyone is singing their part, and each part is as important as the next. It's moving all the time. Harmonizing. Shifting back and forth from bass to tenor to high alto. All of Earth harmonizes. And when God's people come together in harmony—when we are unified, singing our assigned parts—we touch God.

You can't have any one of those three elements alone and call it music.

I always said to my teenage kids, "If I can't whistle it, I don't want to hear it in this house." I still have a little bit of a problem with that, because a lot of music that has come along recently is nothing more than *thump, thump, thump,* as far as I'm concerned. But on the other hand, they have ears to hear that stuff differently than me. I can't hear it, because I wasn't raised on it. I was trained differently than they have been trained.

One of my daughters turned on the radio the other day, and she could hear stuff I couldn't hear. It sounded like jumbled craziness to me. But she could whistle it. She could dance to it. She could even harmonize with it—all because she has an ear that's trained to hear it. So, I have to be careful about being too judgmental when it comes to music.

I have discovered something about dancing, also. God has placed rhythm inside each one of us. It's a gift that God has given us. And let me warn you here: If the church doesn't allow the expression of rhythm, our kids will find someplace else that will. You can repress it and push it down if you want to. But if dancing before the Lord—like David did—is not allowed, our children will find an outlet for it by some other means. They will find some other junk music that is far worse than anything you have ever heard in church. They will find it, and they will dance to that junk instead of dancing before the Lord. Either way, they are going to find a rhythmic outlet.

God has created us to be free creatures before Him. He has placed marvelous things inside of us. He wants to set us loose.

UNCUT STONE

Michelangelo, the great Italian sculptor, said, "The finished form always exists within the uncut stone. The sculptor need only release it."

Every one of us is an uncut stone. When the Master Sculptor gets hold of us and chips away all the stuff that is hiding the real thing He has placed within us, we become God's sculpture.

I remember the first time I went to the Western Wall, also called the Wailing Wall, in Jerusalem. I was so intrigued by the Orthodox rabbis who were there. They go down to the wall, stand in front of it, and pray. But they don't stand still. Their prayers involve a lot of movement. I have since learned that motion-prayer seems to be built into all Orthodox Jews. They can't pray and hold still. Jews don't kneel; Christians do that. Jews pray in motion. They move in different ways, leaning forward, moving up and down. They have their prayer shawls on, and they are in constant motion.

I remember asking an old rabbi at the little gate that goes down to the Wall, "Why do they pray like that?"

"You Christians," he said, shaking his head. "You don't understand. You say prayers. We Jews, we pray with everything that is within us."

Oh, to let everything that is within me praise the Lord!

Nowadays I have real trouble praying if I can't move. I wander around when I pray. I *have* to move. There is so much going on inside of me when I am praying, I just can't remain still. I have to express myself physically when I'm in prayer. It's the reason I think God wants you to get alone when you pray—so you won't accidentally hit somebody in the head.

The gift of movement is inside every one of us. It's who we are. It's the basis of our relationship with the living God. He is a God of movement—and we should be willing to respond likewise. We don't have to go crazy. In fact, I'd warn against being "out of control." But we have to do more than just sit stoically and try not to fall asleep during our prayers.

"IT MIGHT HAVE BEEN"

I remember one of the times I went out on the golf course in Vero Beach to watch my dad's business partner play a round of golf. I was about nine years old. My dad had built our house on some acreage adjacent to a country club in the little town of Vero Beach, Florida. I was born and raised in that house, which bordered the third fairway.

My father's business partner was John W.E. Wheeler, who was 5'1" tall and as bald as a billiard ball. He was a graduate of Purdue University, and he had come down to Florida to go into the citrus business with my father. The two also formed an insurance partnership called Buckingham-Wheeler Insurance Company. Mr. Wheeler ran the insurance company, but every Tuesday afternoon he would go out to the golf course and play 18 holes.

I always enjoyed watching him play. He wore knickers and a little checkered tam o' shanter hat on top of his bald head. He was the most methodical golfer I have ever seen.

He had the exact same routine every time he prepared to hit the ball. He would stand up on the tee box and line the ball up the same way every time. Then he would hit the ball the same way every time: straight left arm, back swing, and *smack!* That ball would fly off the tee 100 yards. Never 90. Never 110. Always

100 yards, right down the middle of the fairway. Then he'd walk down the fairway, pull out his iron, and hit the ball the same way again. It was so predictable!

On this particular day, Mr. Wheeler was on the sixth tee box. He teed up the ball just as he always did. He lined it up and he addressed the ball, shaking his shoulders a little to get himself comfortable. He did everything the same way he had always done it. Then he drew back and swung the club, just as he always did. But this time, instead of the ball going only 100 yards, it went 220 yards, right up onto the green. The ball continued to roll up to the edge of the hole and stopped, barely hanging on the lip of the cup.

Mr. Wheeler turned and looked at me. He took his hat off and said, "Jamie, lad, you have just seen the real John W.E. Wheeler."

Inside every golfer is a Jack Nicklaus or an Arnold Palmer. Inside of every basketball player is a Michael Jordan or a Magic Johnson.

I play basketball with my kids. I used to play a lot of basketball. I used to be able to jump up and, even at my height, dunk a ball. Nowadays, everything in me goes up, but my feet don't leave the ground. But it's still there. I know it's still there. I go up and I come down. It's just that my feet feel like they are nailed to the floor.

But inside of me I am still who I used to be. I am still who I am going to be. There's a fire in my bones—because I am becoming the man God intends for me to be.

That's salvation.

How do you get there? You get there by way of the cross. The tragedy is there are those of us who are not willing to go that way. They refuse to go the way of the cross. They are not willing to pay the price. They are not willing to make the leap. They are not willing to come off the top rail of the fence and see if those dreams of adventure are really meant for them. They are not willing to see if they can fly.

God has placed His desire into each of His children. It's within me and it's within you. God wants every one of His children to be miracle workers. He wants every one of us to be healers. He wants every one of us to give away as much money as the wealthiest person in the world. He wants to flow His prosperity through us.

The problem is we want to keep it all for ourselves. And because we hold on to it, He knows He can't trust us with it. So, He doesn't give it to us.

You will never have anything more until you start giving it away. There will never be an answered prayer until you pray. There will never be a healing until you touch someone and pray for them. You will never speak in tongues until you utter the words. You can sit around from now until Jesus comes, waiting for something to happen, but it won't happen until you move. You have to cooperate with God.

God has created us to be cooperative creatures. He'll not override the strong will that you have. He wants your will to be His will. When you say, "I'm ready for my will to be Your will. If necessary, I am willing to be a fool for Jesus' sake," then wonderful things will begin to happen. The tragedy is that too many of us are afraid to pay the price.

John Greenleaf Whittier, that marvelous American poet, wrote a little poem called "Maud Muller." It's a simple little story about a rich county judge who is riding his horse through the countryside when he sees a young milkmaid. He asks her for a drink of water, and she passes him a cup. He then thanks her, and she smiles at him. Then he rides away. But as he goes, he looks back and thinks to himself, *Ah, that's the woman for me.*

The maid goes on about her chores, and she, too, thinks, *Oh, that's the man for me.* But, afraid to speak, perhaps afraid of rejection, neither one of them says anything to the other about their thoughts.

The judge later marries a climbing socialite and is unhappy all his life. The maid marries a drudge of a farmer, and she's unhappy all her life.

Whittier closes his poem with words that you may have memorized when you were in the seventh grade:

For of all sad words of tongue or pen,
The saddest are these: "It might have been."

Don't let those words be written on your tombstone. God intends for your dreams to come true, but you must pay the price for it to happen. You must run the risk of failing. Run the risk of being a fool. Let that fire that Jeremiah talked about, the fire in your bones, come out. Let it out.

THE BAPTISM

Several years ago, I was invited to speak at a CFO gathering in Kentucky. CFO stands for "Camp Farthest Out." It was one of the forerunner groups of the charismatic movement started by Glenn Clark and Rufus Moseley.

Clark, who was an English professor and a football coach, had a dream that people could be greater than they are. He used to say, "You have to go beyond where you are," which is why he called his little organization "Camp Farthest Out." People would get together, and he would lead them in what he called "devotion in motion." They would sing hymns and sway their bodies along with their hymns. "Open my eyes that I may see . . ." And then they would have their devotions.

The CFO meeting was a three-day event held at the Kentucky Baptist Assembly Grounds near Cedarmore. We had about 300 people attending, and I was speaking on water baptism. There were Episcopalians and Roman Catholics and Presbyterians there, and I thought, *I'm going to have a good time talking about water baptism with these folks.*

I decided that I was going to stretch them a little bit. So that morning I talked about what the Scriptures have to say specifically about being baptized—submersed in water. I told them this wasn't an initiation. If you follow God's direction and you are willing to be baptized in water, God will do something special in your life. Baptism is a step of obedience, one of several in your walk with the Lord. Other steps include being baptized in the Holy Spirit and receiving the gifts of the Spirit. All of these are steps in the salvation process—the process of being transformed into His image and becoming who God wants you to be.

After I had finished my message, four people were waiting for me at the door. "We'd like to be baptized," they said. "We are Episcopalians, and we don't think our priest will baptize us. Would you baptize us?"

I felt like Philip and the eunuch: "Look, here is water. What can stand in the way of me being baptized?"

"Sure, I'll be glad to baptize you," I said. "I'll check around and find out if the stream that runs through the campground is suitable."

I found the camp administrator and told him what we wanted

to do. He said, "That's fine. We have water baptisms down there all the time." So, I went back to the lunch hall where everyone was gathering and told the folks, "We're going to have a baptism service down at the stream at 2 p.m. Everyone is welcome to come and witness it."

As I was leaving, I saw the camp administrator standing in the doorway. "I was a little uneasy about this," he said, "so I made a telephone call to my boss. He said you can't use the stream. It's on Baptist property, and since you are not Baptist, you can't use it. We only allow Baptists to be baptized in our stream. He doesn't know whether this is some kind of alien immersion, or what."

"Okay, so now what am I going to do?" I asked him. "I just told all these people we are going to have a baptism service at 2 p.m., and you're telling me we can't use the water that runs through your camp?"

Then he offered an alternative. "Well, just below the camp, right beyond our property line, the stream empties into a little pond. You can baptize there. It's off our property."

That's fine, I thought to myself. *It's still Baptist water, because it comes through your land. But maybe it changes color by the time it gets to the spillway.*

I went back to the people and said, "We are making a change. We're going to meet a little further downstream, where there's a little pond. Just follow the path, and you will find it."

So, I and the four people who wanted to be baptized changed clothes then walked down to the pond. When we arrived, we saw that everybody from the camp was there—all 300 of them. They were all standing around this little pond, completely encircling it, and they were excited. Most of them had never seen a water baptism service before.

I took the four who were to be baptized and we slowly, carefully, waded out into the water. Boy, was it cold! I mean, it was freezing cold. Then again, it *was* Baptist water.

Anyway, it was very cold, and I didn't know how long I could stand being in it. So very quickly, one by one, I immersed the four people: "In the name of the Father, and the Son, and the Holy Spirit."

As I brought the last person up out of the water and started to step out of the pond, I looked up. There was a man sitting on the bank, pulling his shoes off.

"Wait just a minute," he said. "God just spoke to me. I'm to be next."

"Well, come on, brother," I said. So, he waded out to me, and I baptized him.

As soon as I got him out of the water, I saw four more people stepping into the pond. Then others started coming from all around. They were coming from all directions. I mean, the Spirit of the Lord came on that place! Folks were standing everywhere, waist deep in the pond, waiting their turn to be submersed. By the time we finished, I had baptized almost 100 people.

Something powerful was taking place. It was revival. It was real revival!

Eventually everybody was back out of the water. Folks were standing around dripping wet, shivering, and praising God. Some of them had their hands up. Some were shouting. Others were hugging each other.

I was about to follow them out of the water when a particular woman caught my eye. She had waited until everyone else had been baptized. I had spoken to this woman the day before. She was from Louisville—a wealthy socialite widow of the Kentucky

Derby-Mint Julep set. She was dressed impeccably with the finest clothes and lots of diamond rings and gold bracelets. Her beautiful silver hair was perfectly coiffed. She was about 60 years old, I guessed.

I watched as she began to pull her shoes off. She laid one down gently on the bank, then pulled the other one off and placed it right beside the first. Then she took her purse off her arm and set it down. Next, she removed her beautiful Cashmere jacket and laid it on the ground. Then, here she came, out into the water— diamonds, gold, everything.

When she got to where I was standing, I said, "Obviously, you want to be baptized."

"I want more than that," she responded. "I want to die with Jesus. I want to go to the cross with Jesus. I'm ready."

I put my hand on the back of her head, and she grabbed hold of my arm. I lowered her into the water. "Buried with Christ in baptism," I said, "raised to walk in newness of life."

Then, as I pulled her up out of the water, I saw one of the strangest sights I've ever seen at a baptism service. Her beautiful silver hair had come off in the water, and it was floating away.

I looked at the woman and saw that she was totally bald. She had no hair at all. She was just standing there, dripping wet, with a shiny bald head. Quickly, I reached out and grabbed what was obviously a wig and handed it to her. She took it and just plopped it down on her head. Then she said, "Hallelujah!" and took off out of the water.

Several of the folks standing around on the bank knew her, and they helped her out of the pond. They gathered around her and hugged her and took off up the path back toward the camp, shouting and singing and praising the Lord.

I stayed back in the water for a while, forgetting the cold, watching all that was going on. It was glorious!

That night in the cafeteria, the lady from Louisville stepped in line behind me. She was back to being dressed in her normal way. She had on a beautiful dress, Gucci shoes, and lots of diamonds and gold. Her hair—or wig—was perfectly in place.

"I guess you are wondering what happened this afternoon, aren't you?" she asked politely.

I said, "Ma'am, I haven't thought about anything else."

"My husband died 15 years ago," she began. "I was 45. The morning after we buried him, I woke up, and all my hair was on my pillow. It had fallen out during the night—every strand. I haven't had any hair since. But nobody has known it, because I am wealthy enough to buy the finest wigs."

She paused for a moment, then continued. "Deep down inside, I've wanted to be real. But I haven't known how to be real. There's nothing wrong with someone wearing a wig—except in my case, I was wearing it to hide who I really was. I don't want to hide anymore. When I was down there watching all those people being baptized, I heard God say, 'Now is your time.' I knew that wig was going to come off in the water. But I also knew that was the only way I was ever going to go with Jesus to the cross."

The only way you can ever really have your dreams fulfilled is to go with Jesus to the cross. Only then will all the wonderful things God has placed in your heart come out and take flight.

I want to invite you to lay your life down before Christ. Give Him everything. That includes all your dreams and all your ambitions, all your wants and all your desires—even those you believe to be God-given dreams and desires. I want you to lay them all down and trust God to resurrect only that which He desires for you to keep.

If you will do that, I can guarantee you something. If you will sincerely lay it all down at the cross, I believe that everything you think is missing in your life will begin to come into place.

If you will give everything to God—*everything*—then that thing you have been hoping and waiting for will come to pass. The dream God placed in you will come to pass. But it will only happen through a total surrender of your life to Jesus Christ. It will only happen if you've been crucified with Jesus, buried with him, and raised to walk in a new kind of life.

How it happens is God's business. *When* it happens is God's business. But if you cooperate with Him, He will take care of the rest.

The invitation is very simple. Are you willing to say, "Today, I totally sell out to Jesus Christ. I will not be held back by tradition, or influence, or sin, or fear of what other people think. I will lose all of that, and I will go and do whatever God tells me to do in order for His will to be accomplished in my life"?

Be willing to take that step. Go to the cross. Be the kind of person God wants you to be. Do whatever He wants. Cooperate with Him. Do whatever it takes. Do not hold back.

If you do that, God will honor your obedience, He will honor your pledge, and the Holy Spirit will lead you into new adventures. Your dream of soaring to new heights—like flying with the wild goose—will come to pass, and you will become the new creation in Christ you were always meant to be.

CHAPTER 5

NEW WINESKINS

I am so grateful to have been able to speak to you these past few days. I was eager to come to your church this week, not only because I knew something of what has been happening here, but because I wanted to learn from you, as well.

Whenever I've been gone for a while, the people in my church are a little leery of my return, because I often bring back marvelous new ideas—things we haven't thought of before. I often upset the apple cart, because I want to stretch our ministries and our people beyond their comfort zones. If you think I've been stretching you here these past few days, you ought to be around me all the time.

I believe God wants to establish a relationship between us. I don't know how that is going to happen. I suggested to your pastors this morning that it is time for this church and the entire body of Christ to stretch ourselves beyond our denominational circles. For instance, I have a friend who happens to be a Roman Catholic priest. He is Spirit-filled, and he knows more of the Bible than most Protestant preachers do. I know that's a little threatening, perhaps even a little scary, but it's time we all expand ourselves outward, beyond our denominational walls, and get to know the larger body of Christ.

God is doing something amazing in His kingdom. He wants His people to expand themselves, to expand their minds, without judging others of different denominational backgrounds. Everyone needs the opportunity to approach God at their own speed and in their own manner, without holding back because somebody else is slower or is doing it in a different way than they are used to.

I believe God really does honor the priesthood of every believer. He wants you to approach Him as an individual. The exciting thing about being part of a church like this—and I'm part of one down in Florida—is that we can have folks who show up in coats and ties sitting right next to folks who show up wearing t-shirts and flip-flops. Everyone is welcome. We say, "Brother, we really don't care what you look like on the outside. Sister, it's okay. Come on in. The Holy Spirit is here."

We're not here to correct anybody. The Holy Spirit does a marvelous job of correcting us in His timing. Our task is to forgive and to accept.

Most of the people I run into are already so beat down by the "correctors" in the church that they are cowed, even intimidated. They need somebody who will pick them up and give them a vision of hope. They need someone who will speak to them from the Word of God and tell them they are important to God. They need someone who will say, "You can make it, and we're here to help you do it."

God will put us in our right minds. It's not our task to do that. That's God's business. Stop being so critical.

Besides, you may be dressed more like Jesus than I am. I don't think Jesus would have worn a tie like I did tonight, although I've got some friends who would disagree with that.

I walked out of our hotel room this evening without a tie on. I said to Jackie, "Tell me if you don't like what I'm wearing." My wife, who has a way of pulling her glasses all the way down on her nose when she disagrees with me, said, "I am not going to say anything. I'm not here to correct you. God will correct you."

So, I went back in the room and put a tie on. But way down deep in my heart, I don't think Jesus would dress like this. I'm just conventional enough not to try to stir things up too badly, that's all.

A SPIRIT OF MOTION

Every time the Holy Spirit is mentioned in the Bible, He is mentioned in the context of movement. Movement. There is no mention of the Holy Spirit aside from movement. He is not stable. You need to understand that. If you want to be filled with the Holy Spirit, you need to expect that you will be in motion. You'll be in motion when you worship. You'll be in motion when you pray. You'll be in motion as you grow in the Spirit. You won't be able to stay still.

As I mentioned before, I pastored a Southern Baptist church in Greenwood, South Carolina, for eight years back in the mid-1960s. Once we left there, we did not return for many years.

One Saturday night I was speaking in Charleston, South Carolina. Jackie was with me, and our plan was to leave Charleston the next morning—Sunday—and drive to our little cottage in the mountains of western North Carolina for a short vacation, since we would be relatively close by. I had lined up a special speaker to be at our church back home.

As we were leaving, I decided it would be good if we detoured through Greenwood, which is about halfway between Greenville, South Carolina, and Augusta, Georgia.

We left Charleston early enough to arrive at the South Main Street Baptist Church in Greenwood for the morning worship service. I had not been there in twelve years. Walking into that sanctuary was one of the weirdest experiences I have ever had. Nothing had changed. Nothing. We'd been gone for twelve years, and the same fellows who used to do all the ushering were still there. They never came in during the service. They always hung around outside the vestibule. They sat on the steps and smoked cigarettes during the worship service.

We got there a few minutes late, and there they were—only now they were older and fatter and balder. But it was the same group of men, twelve years older, still doing the same thing.

We approached the front doors, and the ushers found us a seat in the back of the sanctuary. I looked around the congregation, and everybody was sitting in the same place. Twelve years later, I could spot them. Everyone's hair was grayer—or they had lost it. They had grown broader. They were more wrinkled. But all the people were still in the same pews they'd sat in a decade earlier.

The pulpit and the platform furniture were all the same. The choir robes were the same. The music was the same. Nothing had changed.

After the service, I mentioned this to one of the folks. "Nothing has changed," I said. And he said, "Yes. We're stable."

I thought, *You're stable like a cemetery*. Nothing moves there, either. Everybody's facing in the same direction, all laid out, dressed nicely, looking up.

God intends His church to be in motion. He wants you to sing new songs. He wants you to change things—not simply for the sake of change. But if you're going to follow the cloud, as the children of Israel did, you have to move. You have to change.

There's a marvelous passage in the last chapter of the book of Exodus having to do with the children of Israel staying under the cloud. The cloud represented the presence of God, and when the cloud moved, they moved with it. When the cloud didn't move, they didn't move; they set up their tabernacle and stayed put.

But they were only allowed to stay as long as God was there. When God moved someplace else, they had to follow Him. It was Moses' job as their leader to get up every morning, walk out of his tent, look up, and see if the cloud was still there. If the cloud was gone, he shouted to the camp, "Let God arise and His enemies be scattered!"

That was the marching cry for the children of Israel when the cloud had moved. God was saying, "I'm going before you. Follow Me."

Our enemies will be scattered, because God is out there, moving ahead of us. God wants us to be on the move. He wants His church to be mobile and prepared to move.

If you reach out into your communities, you're going to be stretched far beyond anything you ever believed could happen. You will have people with AIDS and all sorts of other illnesses showing up, because they can't go anyplace else to receive the healing of God. You will have the dying and the drug addicts and the drunkards and everybody else coming in, because they will be welcome among you, when they're not welcome anywhere else. And when they come, even though they may be sick or smell badly, God will touch them. He will be the one to clean them up and straighten them out in His timing. All we need to do is be ready to follow the Lord. He will prepare the way ahead of us.

A SPIRIT OF GROWTH

Following the Spirit is going to stretch you beyond your comfort zone, and it will be good, because Jesus will be there. Look at this verse in Mark 2:

> No one sews a patch of unshrunk cloth on an old garment. If he does, the new piece will pull away from the old, making the tear worse. (Mark 2:21)

Draw a circle around that verse. It's a stretching verse for those of us interested in everything the Holy Spirit has for us.

Jesus was in a conversation with the religious people of the day—the Pharisees, the fundamentalists, the Orthodox—and they were trying to nail him down on the subject of fasting. Fasting was a Jewish tradition. Jesus fasted, and I believe He intends for us to fast. It's a discipline that every Christian should be involved in. Last year, I decided I would not eat on Sundays. Every Sunday was a fast day for me. Then, during the 50 days before Easter, I did an extended fast for that entire period.

Jesus believed in fasting, and He wants His people to fast. He upset the Pharisees, however, because He didn't follow their strict rules on fasting. Sometimes Jesus didn't fast on the days the religious people said were set aside for fasting. Other times, He fasted on days that were *not* specifically set aside for fasting.

So, the Pharisees in Mark 2 tried to trip Him up on the details. They stated that John the Baptist and his disciples fasted properly, as did all the Pharisees.

Now John's disciples and the Pharisees were fasting. Some people came and asked Jesus, "How is it that John's disciples and the disciples of the Pharisees are fasting, but yours are not?" (Mark 2:18)

It was then that Jesus gave His odd little answer about unshrunk cloth on old garments.

You seamstresses understand that, don't you? I don't use a sewing machine. Sometimes I sew on a button, and much to my wife's chagrin, I sew up holes in my socks. She thinks I should just throw the socks away and get new ones, but I think they're still perfectly good socks. They just have holes, so why not sew them up?

I don't know much about patches. I do know, however, that if you're going to sew a patch onto something, you have to pre-shrink the patch first, just as the clothes with the holes have already been shrunk. The new patch has to go through the same process that the clothes have gone through, before it can be sewn in.

Jesus also responded with a truth involving the making of wine:

And no one pours new wine into old wineskins. If he does, the wine will burst the skins, and both the wine and the wineskins will be ruined. No, he pours new wine into new wineskins. (Mark 2:22)

I do know something about *this* process, because I've seen it happen in the Middle East. I've drunk out of wineskins in the desert. It's an interesting experience. Believe me, they smell horrible!

In order to make a wineskin, you need a goat's stomach. After the goat has died of some undetermined cause, the stomach is removed. It naturally has openings on either end to allow what goes in to go in and what goes out to go out. During the curing process, these openings are sewn and sealed.

A cured stomach sack is fairly large. You can take it down to the local well and fill it with water, then put a rope around it and carry it over your shoulder. Or, you can fill it with wine. But the stomach skin, or wineskin, will grow old after a while if it's not properly taken care of. It has to be oiled occasionally, and it's best if it is kept filled all the time. If you let it just hang out in the sun, not being used, it'll grow stiff and unyielding.

In this verse, Jesus was drawing a picture. If you pour new fermenting wine into one of these goat-stomach wineskins, the wine will begin to expand. And as it expands, it will stretch the wineskin. If the wineskin is old and stiff, the new wine inside it will cause it to crack and burst open.

I learned a few things about wine after I left the Baptist church. I didn't know much about it before then. I knew some people who I suspected knew a great deal about wine and other alcoholic beverages, but they all pleaded innocent when around me, their pastor. But since leaving the Baptist church, I've learned a thing or two that has helped me understand this verse.

One thing I *did* know is that new wine expands. I learned that back in my days at Mercer College, when my roommate and I attempted to make wine out of lime juice. Lime juice wine! We got a half-gallon ceramic jug with a big cork in the top. We filled that thing up with lime juice and then put in some sugar and some yeast. That was what my friend from the hills of North

Carolina had told me to do. Then we set it in a closet so it would age correctly and become fine wine.

Well, it didn't age correctly. Instead, it exploded! It blew up all over my clothes and my roommate's clothes, and it blew half of the wall out of the back of the closet. People came running out of their dorm rooms, and before long the whole campus knew what we had been up to.

When that thing went off in the back of my closet, I suddenly learned something about wine's expanding qualities. Our mistake was that we needed a valve in the top. The cork was in too tight, and there was no way for the internal pressure to be released. So, *boom!*

Jesus said if you pour new wine into an old wineskin, you're going to be in trouble. All the people He was talking to already knew that, so He just said, "Don't do it." Don't put new wine into old wineskins. If you do, the wine will burst the skins, and both the wine and the wineskins will be ruined.

Jesus simply reminded them, "You need to pour new wine into new wineskins." Find a new, unused goat stomach that still has a lot of expandable, flexible qualities to it. New stomachs can be filled, and they get bigger and bigger and bigger. Old stomachs will simply blow up on you.

What was Jesus really talking about here? Remember, He was saying all this to the Pharisees—the highly religious people of the day. What He was telling them was that God was not going to visit them. God was not going to pour His Spirit out on them, because they were like old wineskins. They would be totally incapable of handling the newness of the Holy Spirit when He arrived. The new wineskin was the still-to-come, newly formed church.

Then he said to them, "The Sabbath was made for man, not man for the Sabbath. So the Son of Man is Lord even of the Sabbath." (Mark 2:27-28)

The law was given to help man, Jesus told the Pharisees. Mankind is not here to serve the law; the law is here to serve mankind. The Pharisees represented old wineskins, and they had it all wrong. Fasting is good and correct, but it is for man's benefit. Man does not fast in order to keep the law.

According to Jesus, the Pharisees were keeping the law simply because it was the law. They weren't keeping the law because it was right or good to do so. They had stopped hearing from God. They had taken God completely out of the equation.

God is saying to us today, "I want to pour out My Spirit upon people who will hear Me, who will expand, who will change, who will walk with Me in faith—not because it's the law, but because they love Me and want to glorify Me."

A SPIRIT OF CHANGE

Every once in a while, down at our church in Florida, I like to change things up. Our folks are like everybody else. They say they're charismatic, filled with the Holy Spirit and agreeable to change, but they still enjoy their ruts. In some ways they are just like the people in my old Baptist church in South Carolina. They have their special seats they like to sit in on Sundays—same side of the room, same row, same chair. They have found a routine, and over the years it has turned into a rut.

My wife also has her special seat. She marks it each Sunday. She comes into the sanctuary, and the first thing she does is put her purse down on her seat so that nobody else will take it while she goes out and greets people.

Once I announced to the congregation, "This is a Sunday for change." *Uh-oh,* I could almost hear the people thinking. Everyone got a little less comfortable. They got itchy and uptight. *What's he going to do now?* they wondered.

"We are going to change it up a little this morning. I want everybody sitting in these two sections to get up and go over there. And I want everybody over there to get up and come over here. You guys cross the aisles and sit somewhere on the other side of the room. I don't want anybody to sit in the same place they are now. You've got three minutes. Now, go. Find your new seat. Get up. Move it!"

Everybody grumbled and complained, but eventually they gathered all their stuff, got up, and found other seats.

Then a remarkable thing happened.

The following Sunday, some of those folks stayed in their new seats. Most of them returned to their old places, and that was fine. They told me later that they didn't want to sit next to the water fountain; they didn't want to sit next to the door. Everybody had a reason for sitting where they did. But several folks came up to me later and said, "Hey, I didn't know it was like that over there." And they found themselves a whole new pasture to feed in for a while.

I've done other things, as well. At one point we reversed the service. For about a year, I did the preaching as soon as everyone got seated, and that was followed by a time of worship. Everybody left the building singing. It was great.

One Saturday I went up to our church with a few friends, and we completely rearranged the auditorium. We were relatively small back then. We still had folding chairs and a lightweight podium. We turned everything around, so that instead of having the pulpit in its usual place on one end of the building, we picked it up and put it on the other end of the building. Then we turned the chairs around so that when the folks came in on Sunday, it was a totally new room. It looked completely backwards.

We can't do that anymore, because we've grown up. We have an expensive sound system that my people won't even let me look at, much less touch or move.

The point is, we ought to be constantly stretching ourselves. We ought to be available for the new things the Lord is telling us to do. Don't wait for God to stretch you. Keep the elasticity going in your own life. Stretch it out.

A SPIRIT OF DISCOVERY

On one of my trips into the Sinai Desert, we were driving across the southern part of the peninsula. We were in a big, old, six-wheel truck with open sides. Our Jewish guide sat up in the front wearing only his shorts and sandals, no shirt. It was hot and dusty, and there were about eight or ten of us cramped into the back of the open-air vehicle. We were driving from one place to another, across this wide expanse of sand, when we approached a *wadi*—a dry riverbed in the desert.

In the southern Sinai, the high mountains are broken up by canyons, or wadis, where the water runs off the mountains and goes in one of two directions. If it flows to the west, the water goes to the Gulf of Suez. If it flows to the east, it eventually ends up in the Gulf of Eilat.

It doesn't rain very often in the Sinai. Most areas only have one inch of rain a year, on average. The problem is that it might be five years before it rains at all, and then you get all five inches in one night.

It's an awesome sight when that happens. The water rushes down those stone mountains and fills up the wadis on its way to the sea. Sometimes you get a wall of water twelve feet high rushing down those steep grades. Everything in its path is swept away.

The wadi we approached was dry and almost a mile wide, but we could see evidence of where the water had come through on several occasions. Our Jewish guide cautioned us to be careful. He said we needed to stay in the ruts of the previous vehicles that had driven through ahead of us. These ruts were obvious, having been there for perhaps several years, since the last rains.

So, obeying his instructions, we followed in the tracks somebody else had made before us.

Once, as we stopped for lunch, I asked him, "Hey, what's that over there, on the side of the mountain? It looks like a big cave in the mountainside."

"Those are old turquoise mines," he told me. "Back during the ancient Egyptian days, before the Exodus, the pharaohs sent work parties down into the Sinai to mine turquoise from the mountains. Those are the remains of those ancient mines."

"Is there any turquoise still in there?" I asked.

"I've heard reports that there may be," he said.

"Can we drive over there?" It was only about half a mile.

He looked at me with a grin and said, "No, I'm not going to do that."

"What do you mean, you're not going to do that?"

"I only drive in the ruts," he said.

"Come on! Just swing over there. It will only take us a few minutes out of our way."

"I'm not going to do it," he said adamantly. "But you can walk over there, if you really want to go."

"I don't understand," I said. "Why won't you drive us?"

Then he told me this story: "Back during the Six Day War in June of 1967, the Egyptians mined this very wadi. It was a major thoroughfare across the Sinai toward Israel, and as the Egyptians were pulling back, they buried land mines everywhere. Today we have no idea where those land mines are, so the only safe way to cross this wadi is to stay in the ruts of somebody who has gone ahead of us.

"When the water comes through here, it uncovers the land mines and pushes them around. Once after a rain a couple of years ago, a Jewish army colonel drove through here and hit a mine. He and his driver were killed. The mines could be anywhere today. We don't know where they are. It's just not safe to drive outside of the ruts."

"I understand," I said, "but I'd still like to go over to those turquoise mines and explore a bit."

"The only way is for you to walk. I'll wait here. When—or if—you get back, we will continue on."

I turned to the other guys who had been listening to this conversation. "Come on," I said. "Let's go."

But after hearing that story, only a couple of them agreed to venture out with me. The others thought it was a good time to take a little rest in the shade of the truck. So, three of us took off on foot to explore the turquoise mines in the mountains.

As we stepped out of the truck, we began to walk very carefully, gingerly. We looked cautiously at every step we took. One of the guys found a big stick, and he'd throw it out ahead of us. Then we'd walk up to where it landed, following each other's footprints, and he'd throw it out again. Eventually we got to the side of the mountain and were able to explore one of the caves. Inside were small pieces of ancient turquoise. They were amazingly beautiful. I even put a few pieces in my pocket to show the others who had remained back in the safety of the truck.

When we returned, the others were impressed by the beauty of the stones. I could almost hear wild geese flying overhead.

I think God wants His people to be adventurers, explorers, discoverers. And let me say this as gently as I can: You'll never find any turquoise unless you're willing to lose a leg to get it done. You'll never move on with God unless you're willing to run the risk of losing your reputation, your job, your money—or maybe a lot more than that.

I know people who've lost their jobs because they've moved on with God. One man in our church told me that his decision to be led by the Holy Spirit meant he could no longer double dip on his expense account, as his supervisor expected him to do. His department had found a way to cheat the company's accounting system without anybody knowing about it. Everyone in the office had to cheat, or they'd all be found out. So, because this man no longer wanted to cheat, he was moved to a different department and later fired.

Things like that happen when you move on with God. You may lose a leg, or a job, or worse. But you'll never experience the new wine unless your wineskin is flexible, unless you're willing to say, "I'll expand this thing! I'll take more of what God has for me, regardless of the cost. I will venture where He leads me to explore."

I had a conversation with my friend Adrian Rogers a couple of years ago. Adrian later became president of the Southern Baptist Convention. But before that, he was the pastor of a Baptist church in Merritt Island, Florida, just fifteen miles north from where we had our tiny start-up Baptist church. Adrian's church, of course, was huge. But we became friends anyway.

Soon after my baptism in the Holy Spirit, I spoke to Adrian about the experience. The whole thing led to him eventually kicking us out of the Baptist Convention, but that's another story for another day.

I quoted Vance Havner to Adrian. Havner was a crusty, old, salt-and-pepper-haired Baptist preacher from North Carolina, who once said, "It's easier to restrain a fanatic than it is to resurrect a corpse."

Adrian replied, "Yeah. But a corpse won't stab you in the back."

"But who wants a church full of dead people?" I said. "I'd rather run the risk of being stabbed in the back by a fanatic than hang around with corpses all the time."

THE BREATH OF GOD

There are two words in the Bible for "spirit." There's a Hebrew word, and there's a Greek word. The Hebrew word used in the Old Testament is *ruach*. It's the same word used for "violent wind" or "cyclone." The Greek word used in the New Testament is *pneuma*. It's the same word used for "wind" and "breath."

Ruach is a strong wind from the outside that moves you by force. The God we meet in the Old Testament is a God who moved people by force. His people didn't always want to go, so He pushed them along.

The God we meet throughout the Bible is a God of progressive revelation. Therefore, you can't take the Old Testament by itself. The Old Testament reveals only a portion of the nature of God. You have to include the New Testament with the Old Testament.

The New Testament is the rest of His story, because God is progressively revealing Himself across history.

That is the reason we have problems with some of the stories from the Old Testament. We don't understand how a loving God can tell His people to wipe everybody out or do other things that seem terrible to us. So, we ask, "Is that what God is like?"

But no, that is not what our God is like. That's only a portion of God's nature. In order to move on with God, we must understand that He has since provided us the potential to be filled and led by His Holy Spirit.

The Spirit of God we see in the Old Testament is the *ruach* Spirit. But when we move on into the New Testament, we discover the Spirit that Jesus talked about: the *pneuma* Spirit. It's the same root from which we take our word "pneumatic." It has to do not with a force from the outside, but a force from within.

Jesus talked about us being filled with the same Spirit He was filled with. If you are filled with His Spirit, you will rise automatically. You will expand automatically. The Holy Spirit we meet in the Old Testament is a Spirit that pushes people. That was necessary in those days. But we never see that aspect of the Holy Spirit in the New Testament, once Jesus came and made His Spirit available to us all.

The Spirit we encounter in the New Testament is a Spirit that comes into our lives and fills us over and over. He gently raises us up at our own pace, as we cast off the weights of life that we have accumulated over time. The more weights we cast off voluntarily, the faster we will rise and mature in Christ. We will rise and we will expand in Him, because He is constantly growing us and maturing us into His likeness.

LED BY HIS SPIRIT

The tragedy for those who are unwilling to grow in Christ comes because Jesus said He will not pour His Spirit into an old wineskin. If you're not willing to stretch or be stretched, if you're not willing to cast off the weights of this world and move forward in newness of life, you will never receive the blessings God has for you. There must be a genuine willingness on your part to be led by His Spirit in order for you to experience the great and wonderful things of God.

An individual must be willing—and the corporate body, the church, must be willing—to move on with God, wherever God wants to move. We don't want to be tomorrow like we are today. We want to expand, grow, mature. God has more for us than to just stay where we are right now. If a church or an individual is not willing to move when and where God moves, God may just go and breathe on some other church or individual in order to have His will be done. But if you are willing to be stretched, if you are willing to pull up your roots and leave your ruts, marvelous things will happen.

Now, along with action and change, sometimes extreme or fanatical things happen. You have to be willing to put up with all of that. When people put off the old things so they can rise in the newness of what Christ has done for them, sometimes their old stuff falls off in unusual ways. Somebody sitting over there may have their old self start to flake off a bit. That's okay, because they desire to move on with God. Relax. Let God work in their life as He sees fit, just as He is working in you.

You may not like how God is working in some of the people around you. But if you're in fellowship with each other, if you are in relationship with each other, it will be okay. You will love each other during the flake-off period. You will believe that they're not going to stay that way, because they're going to rise up. They're going to hit a better atmosphere, a better attitude, a better altitude, as they go up.

I really believe God is telling us to step out. Do the new thing, even if it seems ridiculous.

A close friend of mine named George Sowerby used to be the pastor at a Presbyterian church in Ft. Pierce, Florida, a little town about 45 miles south of where I live. One day George received the baptism in the Holy Spirit. When the Presbyterians found out about it, they threw him out. So, he started a new little independent church in town. Most of his elders and many others from the congregation left with him to start the new fellowship.

For nearly two years, many from that new body drove up the coast every week to attend our Sunday night gathering in Melbourne. Sometimes there'd be 60 of them, all carpooling together, just to be with us for Sunday evening services. They were so enthused to participate in our worship and to see and hear what was going on.

Over that time, George and I developed a close relationship. His wife, Velma, was always at our Sunday evening service, as were two of their three sons. Those two boys were moving in the Spirit. But the third son had gone wayward and was off living a life in the world. He was chasing after drugs and alcohol. George and Velma lost track of him; he just disappeared from their lives. They didn't know where he was or what he was doing.

One Monday afternoon, one of the Sowerby boys, Van, called me. He said that his mom and dad had been vacationing at their cottage in Franklin, North Carolina. His dad had been out the previous afternoon cutting down a pine tree with a power saw.

The tree had fallen in the wrong direction, across a high-tension power line.

George, without thinking, reached down and touched that tree with the still-running power saw. He wanted to complete the cut, hoping the tree would swing loose and fall off the line. Instead, the instant he touched the saw to the tree trunk, he was electrocuted. A high voltage ran down the pine tree, up through the saw, and into his hands. It killed him instantly. The charge was so powerful that it burned holes in the bottoms of his shoes. Apparently, Velma was there with him when it happened.

"Daddy is gone to be with Jesus," Van told me.

Velma called a little later and said, "We're all heading back down to Fort Pierce. We're calling the church group together. Would you come and speak at the memorial service?"

I said, "Sure. I want to do that."

So, Jackie and I went to Ft. Pierce. The little church was meeting in a women's club of some kind, and there were about 100 people attending. They were all sitting in a large circle, which is the way they usually worshiped. There were several rows of chairs around the circle, with the musicians all seated in the first row. They didn't have a piano or organ. They were too small, too poor, for that. Instead, they had guitars.

The service opened, and we began singing. Jackie and I were on one side of the circle, and Velma and her two boys were on the other side. I noticed they held a chair open for Roy, the third son. They had not been able to contact him and tell him what had happened, but they saved a seat for him anyway, just in case he came in. Ever since the accident, the entire family had been praying that somehow God would get through to Roy and let him know that his daddy had died.

We went through the little service, and there was more singing. In fact, there was joyful singing. It was a victory service! It got happier and happier as we got deeper and deeper into worship. Some of the people stood, lifted their hands, and began to shout praises to the Lord.

They had been through a lot as a church. Now, with their pastor gone, they didn't know where they were going. But they stood and praised the Lord anyway.

Soon their little worship band shifted into some lively Jewish songs. A lot of the folks had been to Israel, and they were intrigued with Jewish-style music. Some of them began to dance in place just a little bit. *Wow,* I thought, *dancing at a funeral!* But they were happy. They were filled with joy. Then they began to move into the center of the circle and dance even more.

As all this was taking place, I looked across the circle, and Velma caught my eye. The music was going, everybody was clapping their hands, and we just focused in on each other for a second. I took a step into what was quickly becoming a dance floor, and she met me there in the middle. We hugged, and then we danced the *hora* together.

We both saw him at the same time. He was standing alone at the door in the back of the room. It was Roy. And he was watching his mom and me dance at his daddy's funeral!

Despite what it may have looked like to him, I knew that what we were doing was right. I knew that we were expressing our love for God, and I knew God was pleased. George Sowerby was a man of God, and he'd been taken from us. But God was still on His throne. We were letting everybody know that we believed God was still in control of our lives.

The next time I looked up, Roy was gone.

I spoke for a while, then we concluded the service. After some fellowship time, Jackie and I drove home.

Two years later, I was in Israel visiting a friend named Art Carlson. Art had a ministry called "Project Kibbutz" in which he brought together young people from all over the world to live in community and serve the Jewish people. Many different nationalities of young people moved to Israel and lived for a year on the kibbutz, which was located on Israel's northern border, just a few miles from Lebanon.

Eventually, Art's group formed a little Christian community that got run off by the Jewish government. But it was a very active ministry for many years. When I visited, Art had nearly 150 young people from the United States, Africa, and Europe living on the kibbutz, and he invited me to speak to them.

It was late at night, and all the kids had come together around a great bonfire after a hard day's work. We were out in the open, under the stars. I shared with them a little bit about my life of following the Lord and my experiences living a Spirit-led life.

After I finished speaking, a man and a woman came to me out of the darkness. The young man reached up, put his arm around my shoulder, and said, "You don't remember me, do you?"

I looked at him in the firelight. "No, I guess I don't," I said.

"You were a good friend of my father's. I'm Roy Sowerby, George's wayward son."

I was shocked. "Roy? What in the world are you doing here?"

"I've joined Project Kibbutz," he said. "I'm going to be here for a year. God has called me to be a missionary. I'm getting married soon, and my wife-to-be is here. She and I are going to settle down in Thessaloniki as missionaries to the people of Greece."

"That is marvelous!" I said. "What happened? How did all this come about?"

"You don't know, do you?"

"I have no idea," I admitted. "You are probably the last person I expected to ever see again."

"When I walked into that woman's club the afternoon of my dad's memorial service, I was high on drugs," he began. "I saw you and my mom dancing at my father's funeral. It was then that I knew Jesus was real. When I saw my mom's faith, and how she had risen above everything terrible that had happened, I knew without a doubt He was real. A little later, I made a commitment to follow Him. And this is where I am today—following Jesus."

As far as I know, Roy is still a missionary sharing the gospel to a nation of Greeks. And he is there because his life was changed by simply being open to the leading of the Holy Spirit.

Following God is all about spreading out, expanding your spiritual horizons, letting your Heavenly Father do His thing in your life.

Sure, it's dangerous. Yes, it's risky living. You won't be able to remain seated in the same place you have been for years. Your life *will* stretch and change. But there's no other way to go, if you want to move on with God.

What's the alternative? Stay as you are. Grow stale. Remain in your rut. Never change.

But if you want the turquoise—if you want the good and wonderful things God desires for you to have—step out! Run the risk of being misunderstood. Run the risk of having to sacrifice everything for His purpose. Step out of your rut and follow the leading of the Spirit.

Because that is where the Promised Land is.

Do you want the goodness God has waiting for you? Do you want to be led by the Holy Spirit? Then you have to be willing to lay it all down—your life, your goals, even what you believe to be God-given promises. Everything must be laid down. You must go to the cross and be willing to sacrifice it all for His sake. Whatever the Spirit of God requires, you must be agreeable to His beckoning call.

Are you willing to be led by the Holy Spirit from this day forward? If you are, He will touch you in an incredible way. All the things of this world will have less meaning. The worries of your life will be less important. Your wants and desires will begin to change. Your heart will be tuned to His heart. The fruit of the Spirit—including love, joy, peace, patience, and self-control—will be evident in your everyday life. He will fill you. He will come alongside of you and guide you. He will be with you. And the treasures of heaven will be yours.

Forever.

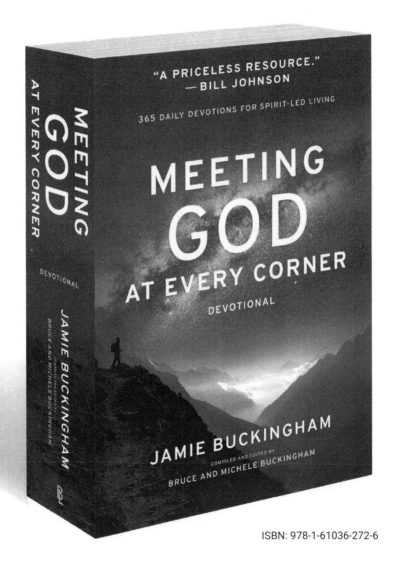

"A PRICELESS RESOURCE."
— BILL JOHNSON

365 DAILY DEVOTIONS FOR SPIRIT-LED LIVING

MEETING
GOD
AT EVERY CORNER
DEVOTIONAL

JAMIE BUCKINGHAM
COMPILED AND EDITED BY
BRUCE AND MICHELE BUCKINGHAM

ISBN: 978-1-61036-272-6

BRIDGE
LOGOS

MEETING GOD
AT EVERY CORNER

"Do not be afraid, for I am with you." (Isaiah 43:5)

I have spoken to many individuals who, for various reasons, are very apprehensive about the future. They seem to be constantly worrying about this or that. But mostly they are anxious about things they have no control over. They wonder what might happen if they lose their job, or their marriage falls apart, or a loved one gets seriously sick—or worse, dies.

People ask me all the time, "What can I do? How can I stop worrying about the future?"

My answer, quite simply, is this: "The only thing you can do when it comes to the future is to trust God."

I tell people that God knows our future, and He has promised to be there when we arrive at it. He knows our worries and our concerns, but He also knows where we are heading. He knows what is around every corner we will turn in life. So, trust Him!

> *THE ONLY THING YOU CAN DO WHEN IT COMES TO THE FUTURE IS TO TRUST GOD.*

There is nothing that could happen to you that God has not seen before. No matter where God leads, others have gone that way before you. In fact, others have been where you *are*, and they have been where you are *going*. As King Solomon said, there is really nothing new under the sun.

God is the same yesterday, today and forever. There may be a lot we don't know about the future; but with God's grace and help, we can make it, just as others did before us. God is there for us, just as He was for them.

I am convinced that whatever happens to us as Christians, wherever God takes us, we will come out on the other side better than we could have ever anticipated or expected.

The word I am hearing for today is faithfulness. Sure, there is uncertainty in the world, but there is also God's faithfulness. There is uncertainty on

MEETING GOD AT EVERY CORNER

man's part, but there is faithfulness on God's part. As the song goes, "Great is Thy faithfulness, morning by morning new mercies I see." [1]

God will not let His people down. His promises are true. He does not lie like men do. He does not do things out of self-interest like men do. God is faithful, and He has made promises to us. He will meet us at every turn.

Life is filled with change—with corners that must be turned. But I'm convinced that if you are walking with God, you can be sure that, around each corner, there is something glorious waiting for you. Every time you make a new turn, life is better in some way than it was before, because God works all things together for good for those who are called according to His purpose.

It doesn't matter what happens to you, because God is already out there in front of you. He'll meet you when you turn that corner. He'll meet you in your times of crisis and in your times of change. He'll meet you when you get married, when you have children, when you change jobs, or when you move across the country. He'll meet you when you are sick, and He will be there, on the other side, waiting for you, when you die.

Great is God's faithfulness! Because of it, we do not have to fear the corners in life—not even the greatest corner, death. We will simply meet Him there, as we always have in life, and move on into what comes next.

Yes, the future is uncertain. But God is in charge of this world. He is faithful. And He will meet you at every corner. Don't be afraid!

---

1   "Great Is Thy Faithfulness" by Thomas Chisholm

STRUGGLE AND REST

"Remember the command that Moses the servant of the Lord gave you: 'The Lord your God is giving you rest and has granted you this land.'" (Joshua 1:13)

Three days before Joshua led the children of Israel across the Jordan River into the Promised Land, he reminded them of the word God had given to Moses earlier. It is a spiritual principle that applies even today: When God fulfills a promise to us, it always comes with a dimension of rest and peace. When God moves you into a new thing or a new place—typically after a lot of struggle—you will know deep inside that God has done it, because you will have peace.

It's true: God's rest and the Promised Land go together.

IT IS THROUGH THE STRUGGLE THAT GOD REFINES YOU.

But before there is rest, before there is peace of heart, you will most likely experience struggle and hardship. Like the children of Israel, in your own quest for a Promised Land, you will go through hardship, struggle, and a period of wandering first.

We tend to resist this. And yet, it is through the struggle that God refines you. He changes you. He makes you more like Him.

Being refined is always circular in pattern, and it never makes sense to our human minds. But God knows, and He understands. Refining is hard. It strains your mind. It's a struggle to circle the mountain. You feel like you're just wandering around, lacking direction. Very often you find yourself experiencing the same difficulties over and over and over again, and you say to yourself, "Haven't I been this way before? Why am I circling this same mountain again?"

Know this: This is the way you reach the Promised Land. You never reach the Promised Land in a straight line.

God could have gotten the children of Israel to the Promised Land in

MEETING GOD AT EVERY CORNER

two weeks. Instead, it took them 40 years. Why? Because God wanted to refine His people. He didn't want them to get to the Promised Land as much as He wanted them to become something different in the process. They needed to be refined through struggle and hardship so that when they reached the Promised Land, they would be prepared to take hold of all that God had for them.

Similarly, the Christian life is a lifestyle of taking up the cross daily, of dying to self. It is a constant dying process. We need to leave behind our old lifestyles and our old ways of thinking—even our old ways of approaching problems—in order to receive God's brand new thing for us. Sometimes that is easy, and sometimes it is incredibly difficult.

There are certain things in our lives that can only be removed by God's refining process—things of tradition that have entrapped us; things of culture that we need to shed. Sometimes the process is simple and obvious. Usually, it's not. It's tough giving up a way of thinking or a philosophy based on cultural acceptance. It's tough giving up something we've always thought was right or okay, but now God is telling us differently.

Take heart in knowing that whenever God walks you through a difficult period of refinement that requires change, it will always be followed by rest and peace of mind. And you will know, deep inside, that it is God—and therefore, it is good.

EXPERIENCING
HEAVEN ON EARTH

Therefore, if anyone is in Christ, he is a new creation; the old has
gone, the new has come! (2 Corinthians 5:17)

We are sanctified through Jesus. We are not the same person we used to be.
We are different. We are changed.

I believe that. I know I'm a different person. Still, it has taken me a long
time to realize that God has not been busy trying to get me into heaven as
much as he has been busy trying to get heaven into me.

For years I have struggled with the theology that says one day we will
"pass through this veil of tears." One day
we will give up this horrible mess we have
made of things here on Earth. One day we
will cross Jordan's icy waters, and there will
be glory on the other side—attainable only
through death.

*GOD DESIRES
TO FILL OUR HEARTS
WITH JOY AND
CONTENTMENT NOW.*

What I am realizing is that God desires
to fill our hearts with joy and contentment
now. His desire is for the kingdom of God
to be in us today. We do not have to wait for that fateful day when we leave
this earth and move into eternity. We can have eternity now—a piece of
heaven on Earth, so to speak.

The blessing of eternity is ours today. The kingdom of heaven is in us
now.

God has commissioned us to proclaim this promise of life, which is
for *today*. We can step out today into joy and hope and peace and all the
things that God has for us. This is the new life that Jesus purchased for us at
great price on the cross. Let's not waste a single moment of it!

My question to you is this: What are you doing with the new life God
has given to you? I am not talking about the physical life you received at
birth. I am talking about your spiritual life—what the Scriptures call "the
abundant life."

MEETING GOD AT EVERY CORNER

As disciples of the Lord Jesus Christ, we are new creatures. When we moved out from under the veil of darkness into the light of Christ, we left behind all negativism and defeatism. We are victorious, and our minds have been renewed to think differently about ourselves and about our lives on Earth.

No longer should we possess negative attitudes or live in fear of death. As Paul told the Ephesians, we are to shake off the old garments we brought with us from the old life. We are to be made new in the attitude of our minds. We are to put on the new garments of our new life in Christ.

God wants to move us from the place of seeing that which is wrong to the place of seeing that which is right. He wants us to leave our old self with its negative attitudes at the cross. He wants us to move from death to life, from the negative to the positive, from defeat to victory.

Think about the new spiritual life God has given you—the life that Christ purchased for you on the cross. Are you bearing fruit? Is your attitude positive? Are you living in joy? Is the outward appearance of your life reflective of your inner peace?

Seek God daily. He will renew your mind and your strength, and you will know that the kingdom of God is within you. Don't wait until you die. All of God's promises are available to you now. Believe God, and experience heaven on Earth today.

JANUARY **4**

WHAT ARE YOU DOING WITH WHAT YOU HAVE?

"So he called ten of his servants and gave them ten minas.
'Put this money to work,' he said, 'until I come back.'" (Luke 19:13)

One of my favorite sayings about material possessions is this: "It's not what you have or how much you have that matters. What matters is what you are doing with what you have."

In Luke 19 Jesus tells the parable of the ten minas. Ten servants were given one mina each by their master. One mina was about three months' wages. Then, each servant was told to put their money to work until the master returned. At that time, an accounting would be made.

God operates by certain principles, and one of them is that if you try to keep the things He has given you, you will lose them. But if you are willing to let them pass through you to someone else, there will be more to come—a great deal more. It is the basic principle of giving. As you give—as you let God's treasure pass through you—

EVERYTHING HAS BEEN GIVEN TO US FOR A PURPOSE.

then God supplies you with more of His treasure, even more than He gave you at the start. But if you refuse to give, or if you are too fearful to give, then you will lose it.

Perhaps it's time we take inventory of what has God given us. Start with the physical things around you, all the things that are here today but could be gone tomorrow—your house, your car, your money. None of these things is permanent.

Next list the "inner things" God has given you. These are the things that make up who you are—your talents and abilities, your giftings, the things you do well.

Jesus tells us to put to work the things He has given us, because everything has been given to us for a purpose. If we choose instead to hide our gifts away or refuse to use them for the glory of God, they become worthless to us. They actually become a hindrance to our spiritual growth. We may very well lose them altogether.

The real danger identified in this parable is the tendency many of us have to not do anything with what God has given us. We are afraid to venture out. We are afraid someone will ridicule us, laugh at us. We are afraid of failure. We say, "What do I know? Let the experts do it. Let the preacher do it. Let somebody else go." We are too afraid to step out and take a risk. That fear is simply a failure to trust God.

Ask yourself, what are you doing to serve the Lord with the gifts He has placed in your hands? What are you doing for His glory? It doesn't matter what your gifts are. All that matters is that you are using them in the way He intends for you to use them. Remember, the power of the Holy Spirit is here to empower God's people to get things done. Don't quench the Spirit by burying His gifts.

Take an inventory of yourself. Who are you? What can you do? What gifts, talents, abilities, resources, and skills do you have at your disposal? Are you using them to bless God? Are you trusting God to grow your gifts for His glory? Remember, one day there will be an accounting. Your God-given gifts are precious and purposeful. Don't let the master return and find that you have buried them in the ground.

DO WHAT GOD CALLS YOU TO DO TODAY

"The wind blows wherever it pleases. You hear its sound, but you cannot tell where it comes from or where it is going. So it is with everyone born of the Spirit." (John 3:8)

When we become Christians and are filled with the Holy Spirit, it becomes God's business to determine what our future holds. It is His business; and like the wind, He goes wherever He pleases. It is not for us to decide what God should or should not do in the future. It is up to Him.

I know many people in ministry who believe they know what God is going to do in the future. They declare themselves to be "prophets." But the Spirit moves and does what only the Spirit knows and desires to do. Nobody really knows where the wind will be blowing in the future. The best we can do is hoist a weathervane and say, "This is the direction it is blowing today."

GOD WANTS US TO EXPERIENCE HIS FAITHFULNESS IN RESPONSE TO OUR DAY-TO-DAY OBEDIENCE.

God is not calling us to see into tomorrow. God is not going to let us know what tomorrow holds. He withholds it on purpose; because if we know what tomorrow holds, we will not do today what He has called us to do today. The very best we can do is to obey Him on a day-to-day basis.

Had I known early in life what was going to happen to me over the coming years, I would not have continued as I did. I would have gone to work planning to bring about what God wanted in my life. I would have set a course of action. I would have gone to a different school or a different church. But that would have spoiled what God had in mind for me and the lessons He wanted me to learn along the way.

My only regrets are that I did not obey God quicker when He began to write things on my heart, and I did not enjoy His blessings afterward. Instead, I spent years struggling, full of anxiety, worrying about tomorrow.

MEETING GOD AT EVERY CORNER

God wants us to experience firsthand His faithfulness in response to our day-to-day obedience. That means we must do today what God is calling us to do today and stop guessing what He may or may not call us to do in the future. God is not going to allow us to feed the hungry of this world until we feed our own children. He is not going to allow us to lead a great ministry until we take care of the ministry in our own households and learn to walk in harmony with our own families.

God measures success by what we do with the things our hands touch today. If He wants to enlarge our success or to end it, that is His business.

God alone is in charge of human history. He is in charge of everything that happens in this nation and this world. We don't get to see into the future, but we can rest assured that no man or force can thwart the purposes of God. His purposes will be fulfilled—and they will be fulfilled in and through you and me if we will obey Him and love Him day by day.

So, don't worry about tomorrow. The wind blows where it wants to blow. Just trust God and do what He is asking you to do today.

Remember the words of Jesus: "Seek first his kingdom and his righteousness, and all these things will be given to you as well. Therefore do not worry about tomorrow, for tomorrow will worry about itself" (Matthew 6:33-34).

ABOUT JAMIE BUCKINGHAM

Jamie Buckingham was an internationally recognized pastor, author, and leader in the Charismatic Movement from the early 1970s to his death in 1992. Respected among liturgical, evangelical, and Pentecostal Christians, he was a close friend and confidant to many of the most influential Christian leaders of the late 20th century.

Jamie wrote numerous books for Katheryn Kuhlman, Corrie ten Boom, Pat Robertson, and many others. His book *Run Baby Run* with Nicky Cruz became an international bestseller. His award-winning magazine columns and bestselling books, including *Risky Living*, *Where Eagles Soar*, and *A Way Through the Wilderness*, cemented his reputation as a transparent, approachable leader, an insightful Bible teacher, and a master storyteller.

Jamie was founding pastor of the Tabernacle Church, an interdenominational congregation in Melbourne, Florida, where he served for 25 years. He lived in a rural area on the east coast of Florida with his wife, Jackie, surrounded by his five married children and numerous grandchildren.

ADDITIONAL RESOURCES

Find books, video Bible studies, workbooks,
audio sermons, and other resources by Jamie Buckingham at
www.JamieBuckinghamMinistries.com